D1520283

DANIEL ORTEGA

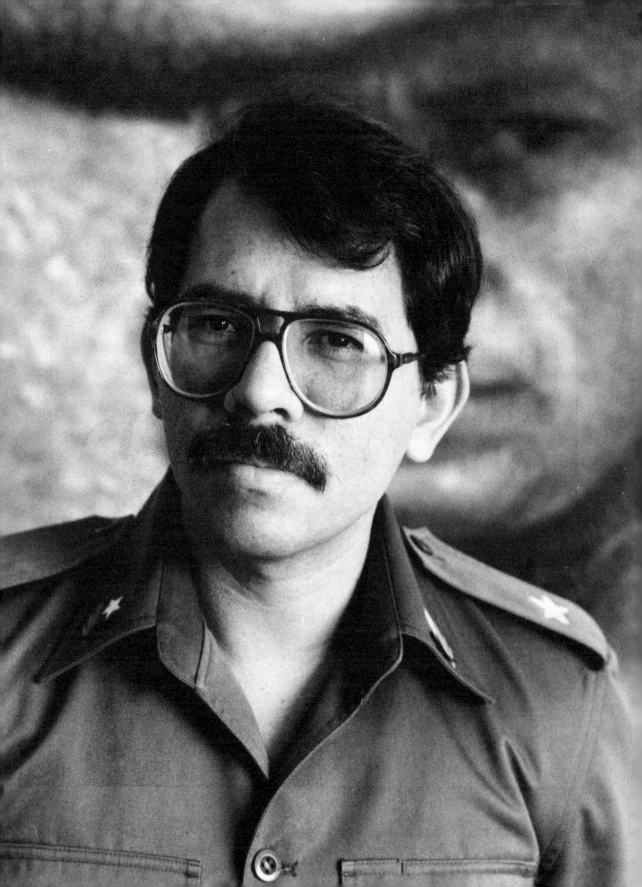

DANIEL ORTEGA

James D. Cockcroft

CHELSEA HOUSE PUBLISHERS
NEW YORK
PHILADELPHIA

Chelsea House Publishers
EDITOR-IN-CHIEF: Remmel Nunn
MANAGING EDITOR: Karyn Gullen Browne
COPY CHIEF: Juliann Barbato
PICTURE EDITOR: Adrian G. Allen
ART DIRECTOR: Maria Epes
DEPUTY COPY CHIEF: Mark Rifkin
ASSISTANT ART DIRECTOR: Noreen Romano
MANUFACTURING MANAGER: Gerald Levine
SYSTEMS MANAGER: Lindsey Ottman
PRODUCTION MANAGER: Joseph Romano
PRODUCTION COORDINATOR: Marie Claire Cebrián

World Leaders—Past & Present
SENIOR EDITOR: John W. Selfridge

Staff for DANIEL ORTEGA
COPY EDITOR: Joseph Roman
EDITORIAL ASSISTANT: Martin Mooney
PICTURE RESEARCHER: Andrea Reithmayr
DESIGNER: David Murray
ASSISTANT DESIGNER: Diana Blume
COVER ILLUSTRATION: Bryn Barnard

First Printing

1 3 5 7 9 8 6 4 2

Library of Congress Cataloging-in-Publication Data

Cockcroft, James D.
  Daniel Ortega/James Cockcroft.
    p. cm.—(World leaders past & present)
  Includes bibliographical references (p.) and index.
  Summary: Surveys the life and times of the leader of the Sandinista
government in Nicaragua.
  ISBN 1-55546-846-2
      0-7910-0682-4 (pbk.)
  1. Ortega, Daniel—Juvenile literature. 2. Nicaragua—Politics and
government—1979– —Juvenile literature. 3. Presidents—
Nicaragua—Biography—Juvenile literature. [1. Ortega, Daniel.
2. Presidents—Nicaragua. 3. Nicaragua—Politics and government.]
I. Title. II. Series.
F1528.22.078C63   1991
972.8505'3'092—dc20   90-19464
[B]   CIP
[92]   AC

Contents

WORLD LEADERS PAST & PRESENT

John Adams
John Quincy Adams
Konrad Adenauer
Alexander the Great
Salvador Allende
Marc Antony
Corazon Aquino
Yasir Arafat
King Arthur
Hafez al-Assad
Kemal Atatürk
Attila
Clement Attlee
Augustus Caesar
Menachem Begin
David Ben-Gurion
Otto von Bismarck
Léon Blum
Simon Bolívar
Cesare Borgia
Willy Brandt
Leonid Brezhnev
Julius Caesar
John Calvin
Jimmy Carter
Fidel Castro
Catherine the Great
Charlemagne
Chiang Kai-Shek
Winston Churchill
Georges Clemenceau
Cleopatra
Constantine the Great
Hernán Cortés
Oliver Cromwell
Georges-Jacques
  Danton
Jefferson Davis
Moshe Dayan
Charles de Gaulle
Eamon De Valera
Eugene Debs
Deng Xiaoping
Benjamin Disraeli
Alexander Dubček
François & Jean-Claude
  Duvalier
Dwight Eisenhower
Eleanor of Aquitaine
Elizabeth i
Faisal
Ferdinand & Isabella
Francisco Franco
Benjamin Franklin

Frederick the Great
Indira Gandhi
Mohandas Gandhi
Giuseppe Garibaldi
Amin & Bashir Gemayel
Genghis Khan
William Gladstone
Mikhail Gorbachev
Ulysses S. Grant
Ernesto "Che" Guevara
Tenzin Gyatso
Alexander Hamilton
Dag Hammarskjöld
Henry viii
Henry of Navarre
Paul von Hindenburg
Hirohito
Adolf Hitler
Ho Chi Minh
King Hussein
Ivan the Terrible
Andrew Jackson
James i
Wojciech Jaruzelski
Thomas Jefferson
Joan of Arc
Pope John xxiii
Pope John Paul ii
Lyndon Johnson
Benito Juárez
John Kennedy
Robert Kennedy
Jomo Kenyatta
Ayatollah Khomeini
Nikita Khrushchev
Kim Il Sung
Martin Luther King, Jr.
Henry Kissinger
Kublai Khan
Lafayette
Robert E. Lee
Vladimir Lenin
Abraham Lincoln
David Lloyd George
Louis xiv
Martin Luther
Judas Maccabeus
James Madison
Nelson & Winnie
  Mandela
Mao Zedong
Ferdinand Marcos
George Marshall

Mary, Queen of Scots
Tomáš Masaryk
Golda Meir
Klemens von Metternich
James Monroe
Hosni Mubarak
Robert Mugabe
Benito Mussolini
Napoléon Bonaparte
Gamal Abdel Nasser
Jawaharlal Nehru
Nero
Nicholas ii
Richard Nixon
Kwame Nkrumah
Daniel Ortega
Mohammed Reza Pahlavi
Thomas Paine
Charles Stewart
  Parnell
Pericles
Juan Perón
Peter the Great
Pol Pot
Muammar el-Qaddafi
Ronald Reagan
Cardinal Richelieu
Maximilien Robespierre
Eleanor Roosevelt
Franklin Roosevelt
Theodore Roosevelt
Anwar Sadat
Haile Selassie
Prince Sihanouk
Jan Smuts
Joseph Stalin
Sukarno
Sun Yat-sen
Tamerlane
Mother Teresa
Margaret Thatcher
Josip Broz Tito
Toussaint L'Ouverture
Leon Trotsky
Pierre Trudeau
Harry Truman
Queen Victoria
Lech Walesa
George Washington
Chaim Weizmann
Woodrow Wilson
Xerxes
Emiliano Zapata
Zhou Enlai

CHELSEA HOUSE PUBLISHERS

ON LEADERSHIP

Arthur M. Schlesinger, jr.

LEADERSHIP, it may be said, is really what makes the world go round. Love no doubt smooths the passage; but love is a private transaction between consenting adults. Leadership is a public transaction with history. The idea of leadership affirms the capacity of individuals to move, inspire, and mobilize masses of people so that they act together in pursuit of an end. Sometimes leadership serves good purposes, sometimes bad; but whether the end is benign or evil, great leaders are those men and women who leave their personal stamp on history.

Now, the very concept of leadership implies the proposition that individuals can make a difference. This proposition has never been universally accepted. From classical times to the present day, eminent thinkers have regarded individuals as no more than the agents and pawns of larger forces, whether the gods and goddesses of the ancient world or, in the modern era, race, class, nation, the dialectic, the will of the people, the spirit of the times, history itself. Against such forces, the individual dwindles into insignificance.

So contends the thesis of historical determinism. Tolstoy's great novel *War and Peace* offers a famous statement of the case. Why, Tolstoy asked, did millions of men in the Napoleonic Wars, denying their human feelings and their common sense, move back and forth across Europe slaughtering their fellows? "The war," Tolstoy answered, "was bound to happen simply because it was bound to happen." All prior history predetermined it. As for leaders, they, Tolstoy said, "are but the labels that serve to give a name to an end and, like labels, they have the least possible connection with the event." The greater the leader, "the more conspicuous the inevitability and the predestination of every act he commits." The leader, said Tolstoy, is "the slave of history."

Determinism takes many forms. Marxism is the determinism of class. Nazism the determinism of race. But the idea of men and women as the slaves of history runs athwart the deepest human instincts. Rigid determinism abolishes the idea of human freedom—

7

the assumption of free choice that underlies every move we make, every word we speak, every thought we think. It abolishes the idea of human responsibility, since it is manifestly unfair to reward or punish people for actions that are by definition beyond their control. No one can live consistently by any deterministic creed. The Marxist states prove this themselves by their extreme susceptibility to the cult of leadership.

More than that, history refutes the idea that individuals make no difference. In December 1931 a British politician crossing Park Avenue in New York City between 76th and 77th Streets around 10:30 P.M. looked in the wrong direction and was knocked down by an automobile—a moment, he later recalled, of a man aghast, a world aglare: "I do not understand why I was not broken like an eggshell or squashed like a gooseberry." Fourteen months later an American politician, sitting in an open car in Miami, Florida, was fired on by an assassin; the man beside him was hit. Those who believe that individuals make no difference to history might well ponder whether the next two decades would have been the same had Mario Constasino's car killed Winston Churchill in 1931 and Giuseppe Zangara's bullet killed Franklin Roosevelt in 1933. Suppose, in addition, that Adolf Hitler had been killed in the street fighting during the Munich *Putsch* of 1923 and that Lenin had died of typhus during World War I. What would the 20th century be like now?

For better or for worse, individuals do make a difference. "The notion that a people can run itself and its affairs anonymously," wrote the philosopher William James, "is now well known to be the silliest of absurdities. Mankind does nothing save through initiatives on the part of inventors, great or small, and imitation by the rest of us—these are the sole factors in human progress. Individuals of genius show the way, and set the patterns, which common people then adopt and follow."

Leadership, James suggests, means leadership in thought as well as in action. In the long run, leaders in thought may well make the greater difference to the world. But, as Woodrow Wilson once said, "Those only are leaders of men, in the general eye, who lead in action. . . . It is at their hands that new thought gets its translation into the crude language of deeds." Leaders in thought often invent in solitude and obscurity, leaving to later generations the tasks of imitation. Leaders in action—the leaders portrayed in this series—have to be effective in their own time.

And they cannot be effective by themselves. They must act in response to the rhythms of their age. Their genius must be adapted, in a phrase of William James's, "to the receptivities of the moment." Leaders are useless without followers. "There goes the mob," said the French politician hearing a clamor in the streets. "I am their leader. I must follow them." Great leaders turn the inchoate emotions of the mob to purposes of their own. They seize on the opportunities of their time, the hopes, fears, frustrations, crises, potentialities. They succeed when events have prepared the way for them, when the community is awaiting to be aroused, when they can provide the clarifying and organizing ideas. Leadership ignites the circuit between the individual and the mass and thereby alters history.

It may alter history for better or for worse. Leaders have been responsible for the most extravagant follies and most monstrous crimes that have beset suffering humanity. They have also been vital in such gains as humanity has made in individual freedom, religious and racial tolerance, social justice, and respect for human rights.

There is no sure way to tell in advance who is going to lead for good and who for evil. But a glance at the gallery of men and women in *World Leaders—Past and Present* suggests some useful tests.

One test is this: Do leaders lead by force or by persuasion? By command or by consent? Through most of history leadership was exercised by the divine right of authority. The duty of followers was to defer and to obey. "Theirs not to reason why / Theirs but to do and die." On occasion, as with the so-called enlightened despots of the 18th century in Europe, absolutist leadership was animated by humane purposes. More often, absolutism nourished the passion for domination, land, gold, and conquest and resulted in tyranny.

The great revolution of modern times has been the revolution of equality. The idea that all people should be equal in their legal condition has undermined the old structure of authority, hierarchy, and deference. The revolution of equality has had two contrary effects on the nature of leadership. For equality, as Alexis de Tocqueville pointed out in his great study *Democracy in America*, might mean equality in servitude as well as equality in freedom.

"I know of only two methods of establishing equality in the political world," Tocqueville wrote. "Rights must be given to every citizen, or none at all to anyone . . . save one, who is the master of all." There was no middle ground "between the sovereignty of all and the absolute power of one man." In his astonishing prediction of 20th-century totalitarian dictatorship, Tocqueville explained how the revolution of equality could lead to the *"Führerprinzip"* and more terrible absolutism than the world had ever known.

But when rights are given to every citizen and the sovereignty of all is established, the problem of leadership takes a new form, becomes more exacting than ever before. It is easy to issue commands and enforce them by the rope and the stake, the concentration camp and the *gulag.* It is much harder to use argument and achievement to overcome opposition and win consent. The Founding Fathers of the United States understood the difficulty. They believed that history had given them the opportunity to decide, as Alexander Hamilton wrote in the first Federalist Paper, whether men are indeed capable of basing government on "reflection and choice, or whether they are forever destined to depend . . . on accident and force."

Government by reflection and choice called for a new style of leadership and a new quality of followership. It required leaders to be responsive to popular concerns, and it required followers to be active and informed participants in the process. Democracy does not eliminate emotion from politics; sometimes it fosters demagoguery; but it is confident that, as the greatest of democratic leaders put it, you cannot fool all of the people all of the time. It measures leadership by results and retires those who overreach or falter or fail.

It is true that in the long run despots are measured by results too. But they can postpone the day of judgment, sometimes indefinitely, and in the meantime they can do infinite harm. It is also true that democracy is no guarantee of virtue and intelligence in government, for the voice of the people is not necessarily the voice of God. But democracy, by assuring the right of opposition, offers built-in resistance to the evils inherent in absolutism. As the theologian Reinhold Niebuhr summed it up, "Man's capacity for justice makes democracy possible, but man's inclination to injustice makes democracy necessary."

A second test for leadership is the end for which power is sought. When leaders have as their goal the supremacy of a master race or the promotion of totalitarian revolution or the acquisition and exploitation of colonies or the protection of greed and privilege or the preservation of personal power, it is likely that their leadership will do little to advance the cause of humanity. When their goal is the abolition of slavery, the liberation of women, the enlargement of opportunity for the poor and powerless, the extension of equal rights to racial minorities, the defense of the freedoms of expression and opposition, it is likely that their leadership will increase the sum of human liberty and welfare.

Leaders have done great harm to the world. They have also conferred great benefits. You will find both sorts in this series. Even "good" leaders must be regarded with a certain wariness. Leaders are not demigods; they put on their trousers one leg after another just like ordinary mortals. No leader is infallible, and every leader needs to be reminded of this at regular intervals. Irreverence irritates leaders but is their salvation. Unquestioning submission corrupts leaders and demeans followers. Making a cult of a leader is always a mistake. Fortunately hero worship generates its own antidote. "Every hero," said Emerson, "becomes a bore at last."

The signal benefit the great leaders confer is to embolden the rest of us to live according to our own best selves, to be active, insistent, and resolute in affirming our own sense of things. For great leaders attest to the reality of human freedom against the supposed inevitabilities of history. And they attest to the wisdom and power that may lie within the most unlikely of us, which is why Abraham Lincoln remains the supreme example of great leadership. A great leader, said Emerson, exhibits new possibilities to all humanity. "We feed on genius. . . . Great men exist that there may be greater men."

Great leaders, in short, justify themselves by emancipating and empowering their followers. So humanity struggles to master its destiny, remembering with Alexis de Tocqueville: "It is true that around every man a fatal circle is traced beyond which he cannot pass; but within the wide verge of that circle he is powerful and free; as it is with man, so with communities."

1

Day of Joy

July 16, 1979 — the hottest time of year in a city that is always hot. As the sun rises over downtown Managua, the capital of Nicaragua, it illuminates a ruined plaza. A ragged, elderly woman scuttles along the street, sidestepping potholes, picking her way through broken chunks of cement, passing weed-covered, vacant lots and the remnants of collapsed buildings.

The woman observes the once-beautiful 18th-century National Cathedral. It looks intact from across the plaza, but its roof is missing. A granite statue of Saint Peter clings to a chunk of stone on the topmost wall. Inside, wild grass has sprouted through jagged cracks in the floor, growing tall around the crumpled piles of wood that once were orderly pews.

We have found a country destroyed. Destroyed by the bombs dropped by Somoza's air force, which bombed out cities indiscriminately. Destroyed as a result of 45 years of plunder by a corrupt regime. In fact, what we have now is a completely bankrupt country: our reserves were plundered; the people's money, down to the last cent, was spent on weapons to use against the people.
—ALFONSO ROBELO
member of the five-person
Junta of National
Reconstruction

A young girl celebrates the fall of Nicaraguan dictator Anastasio Somoza Debayle. The Somoza dynasty, established in Nicaragua by the United States government during the 1930s, finally came to an end on July 17, 1979, when Sandinista guerrillas ousted the hated tyrant.

The National Palace in Managua, the capital of Nicaragua, stands in striking contrast to the squalor surrounding it. For approximately 50 years, the Somoza clan sapped the country's resources through countless abuses of power and left Nicaragua's masses desperately impoverished.

To the right side of the plaza, away from the church, the National Palace stands miraculously unharmed. It is a stark monument to "los muchachos," the young soldiers of the Sandinista Front of National Liberation guerrilla army (FSLN). A year earlier, they had risked their lives to capture its occupants — dictator Anastasio Somoza Debayle's lackey congressmen and government employees — in exchange for the release of political prisoners.

On the blocks around the palace, there remain only empty shells and smoke-blackened walls of what once had been high-fashion boutiques and cafés. With a shudder, the woman recalls the powerful earthquake that shattered Managua just past midnight two days before Christmas 1972, leaving a burning, blacked-out city of ruins with 10,000 dead and at least as many injured. She and the rest of Managua's survivors had been left homeless, without electricity, without drinking water, scavenging for canned goods in the wreckage.

The government's response to the earthquake marked the beginning of the downfall of the hated tyrant Somoza. Little of the international aid rushed to Managua reached those who needed it the most. Instead, the greedy hands of Somoza and his cronies seized it to enrich themselves. Rumored to be worth more than a billion dollars, Somoza already owned a quarter of the richest farmland, the national airline, a bank, a Mercedes-Benz automobile concession, a newspaper, a television station, and 50 of the nation's largest companies, including the cement works. One of his first acts after the earthquake was to raise the price of cement, so desperately needed for reconstruction.

Somoza's son Anastasio Somoza Portocarrero headed up the relief operations. Under his guidance, medical supplies and food were put on the black market, where only the rich could afford them. The National Guard and government employees were awarded special access to the rest of the emergency supplies. Managua's hungry citizenry watched day after day as Somoza rode through the remains of the city in his Mercedes, dressed in white summer suits with silk sashes wrapped around his swollen middle, laughing and cavorting with overdressed women.

The U.S. government had put the Somoza clan in power in the 1930s, arming and training the National Guard that kept them safe. During the earthquake tragedy, the administration of President Richard Nixon still considered Somoza an important ally. Nevertheless, the dictator's thefts were an embarrassment. Even Managua's businessmen, who seldom criticized the 40-year Somoza dynasty, began to complain. When raging fires and mounting piles of corpses made it necessary to evacuate the quake-rocked capital, some of the young men and women made for the hills to join "los muchachos," the FSLN guerrillas.

The woman in the plaza glances nervously up at the distant hills behind the palace and shudders again. Overlooking the city, the luxurious Intercontinental Hotel is intact, its nine tiers resembling a modern imitation of an Egyptian pyramid. Not far

It was obvious to me that I needed a special "storekeeper." In my son Tachito, who was then attending Harvard University, I found the man I wanted. He was not in Managua when the earthquake occurred and, therefore, I felt he could be totally objective in his assigned responsibilities. This assumption proved correct.
—ANASTASIO SOMOZA
on his choice of his son to run the earthquake relief effort

15

A young man, one of the many victims of the Somozas' repressive National Guard, lies in a pool of blood in the Monimbo section of Masaya, Nicaragua, in September 1978. The graffiti reads (left) "National Guard out of Monimbo" and (right) "Because of Somoza, the people are dying."

from it is a much smaller structure resembling a hut or lookout post. It is the entrance to Somoza's "bunker," with its posh offices, prison cells, and infamous torture chambers. He is still holed up in there, Somoza III, with his flashy mistress Dinorah Sampson and his armed bodyguards, the cream of the despised National Guard installed by "los Yanquis"—the U.S. Marines.

For several weeks, Somoza had been hiding out in his bunker while his pilots rained bombs down on factories owned by his opponents, leaving only his own properties intact. The planes dropped their canisters of death on hospitals and schools too, concentrating especially on the working-class districts, where people were supporting los muchachos. After the saturation bombings, National Guard units marched into the devastated neighborhoods, murdering the wounded and those who were in hiding. Teenagers were their favorite targets; the guard was convinced that they were all FSLN "muchachos." The more violent the guardsmen became, the more young people joined the Sandinista cause.

At night, Somoza drank with his mistress, listening to disturbing news on the radio. The streets of six cities were controlled by young people wearing the red-and-black bandanas of the Sandinistas and carrying machetes, pistols, even automatic rifles. Several National Guard units had deserted or surrendered. Worse yet, Somoza could expect no help from his American friends. President Jimmy Carter's special emissary, William Bowdler, was already in Costa Rica negotiating a settlement with leaders of the Junta of National Reconstruction, composed of Sandinista guerrillas and anti-Somoza business leaders. Somoza was advised to resign and leave for his own safety.

Instead, Somoza ordered more bombings. If he was forced to go, he would destroy everything he could not carry with him, leaving as little as possible for the rebels. He had seen to it that his lands were burned so that no one else could make use of the crops. His cattle, more than 2 million head, had been slaughtered and were in cold storage in Miami. The sale of all of that beef would make him even richer and leave Nicaragua a hungrier land. For several years, Somoza had borrowed to the limit from private banks and the International Monetary Fund. His enemies' Junta would be floating in a sea of debt with the world's worst credit rating.

Sandinista rebels, sometimes called *los muchachos* (the boys), shoot from behind a barricade in the streets of Masaya, Nicaragua. Though the Sandinistas ousted Somoza and forced him into exile on July 17, 1979 — the Day of Joy — war continued to divide the country for more than a decade.

By nightfall, Somoza had made up his mind. At about 1:00 A.M., with the distant, muffled booms of mortar shells and crackling of machine-gun fire becoming more audible, the Nicaraguan Congress held a panicky session in a conference room at the Intercontinental. Somoza's letter of resignation was quickly read, and Dr. Francisco Urcuyo Miliano was "elected" as the new president. President Carter's special envoy and other negotiators had arranged for Urcuyo to turn the government over to the Junta of National Reconstruction as soon as it arrived in Managua. But in his speech, Dr. Urcuyo hinted that he would not carry out his part of the bargain.

After the inaugural ceremony, the "guests" — National Guard commanders and the rest of Somoza's government — tossed their overstuffed suitcases aboard buses and military vehicles and made their getaway. Somoza himself gave a rambling emotional speech to his staff at the bunker and squeezed into a limousine for the short ride to a helicopter perched on the hilltop. Behind him a small truck carried the entombed remains of his father and brother, Anastasio Somoza and Luis Somoza. The last news Somoza heard before he left was that the victorious guerrillas were on their way to Managua, headed straight for the bunker. He was getting out just in time.

At Las Mercedes airport, a U.S. Convair 800 flew Somoza and about 100 others out of the country to Homestead Air Force Base near Miami. A Cadillac limo drove Somoza to his yacht for the short hop to his mansion on a Biscayne Bay island, off the coast of Florida.

In Nicaragua, the tyrant Somoza's departure would be celebrated on July 17 for years to come as the Day of Joy. Hours before dawn, in Costa Rica's capital city of San José, fire sirens wailed. A neon sign over the radio station flashed the news, "Thank God, Somoza has fallen." In hotel lobbies, hundreds of Nicaraguans who had fled for their lives from the Somoza dictatorship came down from their rooms to celebrate.

Two of the Sandinista members of the new Junta of National Reconstruction, Daniel Ortega Saavedra and Moisés Hassan Morales, were already in rebel-held León, waiting to travel to Managua for the swearing-in ceremonies. The remaining three Junta members — Sergio Ramírez Mercado, Ortega's friend and a prominent writer, and two represen-tatives of the anti-Somoza business establishment, Alfonso Robelo Callejas and Violeta Barrios de Cha-morro — planned to fly from Costa Rica to Managua as soon as Urcuyo made his arrangements. Instead, they were summoned to an all-day meeting with U.S. negotiators and Latin American officials. They learned that Urcuyo was refusing to resign. U.S. ambassador Lawrence Pezzullo and 20 American Embassy staff members had left Nicaragua in pro-test against Urcuyo's foolhardy actions.

The U.S. negotiators argued against uncondi-tional surrender by the National Guard, hoping that it would remain intact, an armed counterbalance to the victorious Sandinista guerrillas. But the Na-tional Guard troops knew enough to fear for their lives. Most Nicaraguans considered them the worst kind of vermin, murderous enemies of the people. On the morning of Somoza's departure, the soldiers were shedding their uniforms and hiding their weapons. Some, wearing civilian clothes under their uniforms despite the oppressive heat, rushed into the lobby of the Intercontinental Hotel, took off their uniforms and rifles, and ran back outside to mix with the crowds or flee from the city. About 250 fleeing guardsmen and their families hopped on Red Cross food-relief planes and flew out of the country.

All day long, Sandinista fighters advanced on Ma-nagua along two of the three paved highways lead-ing to the capital. As they moved past small towns along the way, men, women, and children joined the guerrillas to fight the last remnants of the Na-tional Guard. It was the last march of a terrible 7-week finale to a guerrilla war that for some Nica-raguans had lasted 20 years — a war that in its final months took the lives of 50,000 people in a nation of less than 3 million.

With the Managua airport in turmoil, the three Junta members from Costa Rica were refused per-mission to land. The pilots of two separate planes were instructed to fly out to sea and then over a beach resort to León's airport. Once the five Junta members were reunited in the temporary capital, León, they issued a final call for unconditional surrender of the National Guard.

In a last-ditch effort to remain in power, Urcuyo dispatched a National Guard convoy to attack the rebel stronghold in León. The convoy was captured a short distance from Managua, and the remaining guard commanders prepared to surrender. They informed Dr. Urcuyo that they were almost out of ammunition and fuel and desertions were climbing.

On the evening of July 18, Urcuyo finally resigned. Three Guatemalan air force planes flew him, his family, and other civilian officials to Guatemala. From Costa Rica, Humberto Ortega Saavedra, brother of Junta leader Daniel Ortega and member of the Sandinistas' nine-member National Directorate, ordered a cease-fire and demanded that Somoza's troops turn themselves and their weapons over to the International Red Cross. In most cases, that had already happened. Ortega promised to respect the lives of guardsmen who obeyed the order.

At police headquarters, 600 prisoners were released and a huge cache of armaments was turned over to the Red Cross. At Nicaragua's air force base, 1,200 troops surrendered peacefully. But on the southern front, about 1,000 guardsmen raced to the port of San Juan del Sur, stole fishing boats and pleasure yachts, and sailed for El Salvador and the friendly protection of its dictator. Another 2,000 or more guardsmen dashed across the northern border into Honduras. From there they were determined to wage a new war against the Sandinistas.

On the morning of July 19, the plaza in Managua began to fill with people dancing, cheering, hugging and laughing. Then the news spread through the crowd — "Llegan los muchachos!" "The kids are coming!" — as the first contingents of the FSLN guerrilla army reached the downtown area, dressed in olive green uniforms, grinning, waving hundreds of red-and-black Sandinista flags, and joyously firing their automatic rifles.

Some Sandinistas marched up to the bunker, entering cautiously, as though they could not really believe that the Somoza family, in power for 47 years, was actually gone. The compound's front offices were empty. Through the open door of Somoza's elegantly furnished office, they saw a painting of his father, Anastasio Somoza García (Somoza I), put in power by U.S. Marines long before the Sandinista guerrillas were born. A mile away, cheering crowds pulled down a heavy statue of Somoza I mounted on horseback. In the newly named Plaza of the Revolution, someone climbed the crumbling wall of the Cathedral and stuck a red-and-black FSLN flag into the stone hand of Saint Peter.

The members of the junta of the Sandinista provisional government — (standing, from left) Alfonso Robelo Callejas, Moisés Hassan Morales, Daniel Ortega Saavedra, Violeta Barrios de Chamorro, and Sergio Ramírez Mercado — are greeted by a jubilant crowd in downtown Managua on July 20, 1979.

It was only the first day of the festivities. Everyone was waiting for the Junta to arrive from León.

The next day, July 20, 1979, the Managua airport bustled with activity. As a DC-3 from Costa Rica flew overhead, the pilot announced: "Welcome to the Augusto Sandino Airport." The passengers — top FSLN leaders and U.S. and Latin American diplomats — applauded and shouted "Viva!" as a welcoming committee of guerrillas fired a barrage of bullets into the sky.

Some 200,000 people jammed into the area surrounding the National Palace and the cathedral as a bright red fire engine, sirens blaring, made its way toward the plaza. Riding in triumph on top of the engine were the five new leaders. They were met by an honor guard of marching FSLN troops. Thousands of shots were fired into the air as the fire engine entered the plaza, followed by a convoy of trucks, tanks, buses, even horses and mules carrying young Sandinista rebels. Some had walked 70 miles from the northern town of Estelí, site of one of the FSLN's most famous battle victories.

In front of the National Palace, the five leaders were introduced to the roaring crowd. They stood before a huge drawing of three national heroes, martyrs to the cause: General Augusto César Sandino, killed on the orders of Somoza I in 1934; Carlos Fonseca Amador, who founded the FSLN in 1960 and was killed in combat in 1976; and Pedro Joaquín Chamorro Cardenal, a newspaper editor murdered in 1978 and the husband of Junta member Violeta Chamorro.

The crowd roared "Cero, Cero!" for Edén Pastora, "Comandante Cero," who led the raid on the National Palace the previous August. Now Pastora had returned to the palace, not as a guerrilla "bandit," but as a member of the FSLN National Directorate.

The Junta's swearing-in ceremony was witnessed by two pillars of the church, Archbishop Miguel Obando y Bravo of Managua and Bishop Manuel Salazar y Espinoza of León. Probably the least known of the five Junta members was the youngest one, Daniel Ortega, age 34. He had joined the revolutionary movement when he was 15. Somehow he had survived not only years in the mountains fighting the National Guard, but also seven years in Somoza's nightmare jails, where he had almost died from beatings and tortures. Over his right eye a deep scar lingered. On this joyful day even Ortega, known for his serious nature, smiled and waved.

He knew the challenges that lay ahead. In a sparsely populated country about the size of Ohio, close to a million people were starving. Rebuilding seemed almost impossible with so many industries destroyed by Somoza and a foreign debt of $3 billion. So many of the Nicaraguan people were homeless; so many children orphaned.

Daniel Ortega nodded gravely as Tomás Borge Martínez, the only living original founder of the FSLN, warned the assembled people that the real struggle was about to begin — "a war against backwardness, against poverty, against ignorance, against immorality, against destruction. This war is more difficult, tough and prolonged than the previous war."

2

Children of Sandino

Our cause will triumph because it is justice and love.
—AUGUSTO CÉSAR SANDINO

Daniel Ortega Saavedra was born on November 11, 1945, in the mining town of La Libertad. Located in the region of Chontales, Nicaragua, La Libertad is more than 100 miles east of Managua. Daniel was the third child born to Daniel Ortega and Lidia Saavedra Ortega. As is customary in Latin America, his middle name, Ortega, is his father's family name, whereas Saavedra, his mother's maiden name, is given last.

Daniel's father, called Don Daniel by almost everyone, was the son of an educator from Granada and a servant woman who had worked for the Ortega family. It was not an uncommon event for rich sons to seduce frightened young housemaids, who were dependent on keeping their jobs, and then leave them to raise a child alone.

Whereas his father supported Somoza I, Don Daniel, growing up in poverty, opposed the tyrant. He married Lidia Saavedra, who also came from a poor family and shared his moral principles. Don Daniel

Augusto César Sandino, leader of Nicaraguan rebel forces during the 1920s and 1930s, waged guerrilla warfare on U.S. Marines in Nicaragua in 1927, seeking to rid his country of U.S. military intervention. As a boy, Daniel Ortega loved to listen to tales of Sandino's courageous exploits.

became an accountant for a mining company in La Libertad. In rapid succession, three children were born to the young couple: Sigriedo, Germana, and then Daniel. The pay was low, and the living conditions were terrible, though not as bad as what the miners faced. When hungry miners stole food from the company store for their families, Somoza's National Guard beat, tortured, and even killed them.

Shortly after Daniel's birth, the gold mines closed down, and La Libertad became a virtual ghost town. Daniel's parents, without savings or job prospects, could barely survive. When the two oldest children fell ill, there was no medical care available, and they died.

Hoping to save Daniel from such a fate, the Ortegas moved to Juigalpa, a larger town closer to Managua. As Don Daniel shifted from one underpaid job to another and back into joblessness, the family was often evicted for nonpayment of rent. In 1947, another son, Humberto, was born.

After moving to Managua, the Ortegas' situation improved only slightly. Don Daniel ran a small import-export business, and his wife opened a neighborhood bakery. Like all of Somoza's opponents, they were constantly harassed by the National Guard. They earned just enough to keep the family fed and the rent paid. In Nicaragua, only those with connections to the dictatorship prospered. Two more children were born — a boy, Camilo, and a girl, Germana — to "replace the two who had died," the Ortegas said.

Only the poorest of the poor attended the substandard public schools in Managua. Daniel and Humberto were sent to Catholic or private schools, never staying in any one school for very long. When tuition came due, they were thrown out because their parents could not pay the bill.

The real education of the Ortega children took place at home, as Don Daniel and Lidia Ortega tried to counter the pervasive American influences on Nicaraguan culture left behind by the 1909–1933 military occupation of the country by the U.S. Marines. Growing up in Nicaragua meant playing baseball, listening to American music, and watching

Walt Disney movies. Many of Daniel's playmates went to sleep at night hearing bedtime stories such as "Peter Rabbit" and "Little Red Riding Hood."

Daniel was not read fairy tales. Instead his parents recounted true stories of Nicaragua's tortured history. Daniel never tired of hearing about the adventures of brave Nicaraguans who through the centuries fought and died to free their homeland. His favorite tales dealt with the amazing Augusto César Sandino.

Sandino was the little "David" who with his mere slingshot had slain the mighty "Goliath" in 1933, driving out the U.S. Marines. Both of Daniel's parents had worked for the cause of their nation's "George Washington." But the story had an unhappy ending. Sandino did not outwit the head of the National Guard installed by the marines to take their place—Somoza I, Anastasio Somoza García.

The Ortega children learned that even before Sandino's time their country had not been free. Numerous foreigners had invaded Nicaragua looking for riches, massacring those who resisted and enslaving those who did not. First came the Spaniards, searching for gold. They found little gold but plenty of hard-working Indians, descendants of those who had arrived from Mexico and the Caribbean a thousand years earlier. Nicaragua was a beautiful land, filled with lakes and rivers that watered lush valleys. The Pacific Ocean hugged one coast, the Atlantic the other. Dotting the Pacific plain from Lake Nicaragua in the south to the Gulf of Fonseca in the north were dozens of volcanoes, whose ashes made the western valleys some of Central America's most fertile. But geological instability also produced earthquakes, and Don Daniel remembered well the 1931 tremor that left Managua in ruins.

Daniel's father told of how his country was named after Nicarao, the Indian chieftain who negotiated the first peace treaty with the Spaniards. But the invading Europeans' treaties were almost never upheld. The Spaniards seized all the lands of the Indians and made them work on them as virtual slaves. Even in the 16th century, Nicaragua had its rebels. One of them, Diriangen, led poorly armed Indians in a bitter fight to the death against the Spaniards. But by 1580, Nicaragua's million or more Indians were reduced by massacre, disease, overwork, and hunger to less than 45,000.

Then came the English. They made the isolated Atlantic coastline of Nicaragua and Honduras a British protectorate. They armed the Miskito Indians as a home army, sending them off to Jamaica to fight slave revolts.

Inland from the coast rose the rain forests and mountains that cut off the Atlantic peoples from the majority of Nicaraguans to the west. The coastal people were usually Protestant and spoke English or Indian tongues. Most of the other Nicaraguans were Catholic and spoke Spanish. About 10 percent of the people were white-skinned descendants of the Spaniards. Almost everyone else was brown-skinned *mestizo*, Spanish-Indian mixed-bloods like the Ortegas themselves.

In their attempts to control Nicaragua, foreign powers often focused on the Atlantic coast. Most of Nicaragua's ethnic minorities lived there. Numbering under 100,000, they were about 70 percent Miskito Indians and 23 percent Creoles, an English-speaking Afro-Caribbean people. There were also a few thousand Sumu Indians and an even smaller number of Rama Indians and Garifuna (Afro-Indians famed for resisting conquest).

Spain's empire fell apart early in the 19th century under the triple blows of British economic power, Napoléon's invasion of Spain, and campaigns by Latin America's "independence armies." Throughout Central America and Mexico, landless Indians, slaves, and mestizos rose up against Spanish-descended whites and churchmen who ruled over them as owners of banks, commerce, and landed estates called haciendas. To keep the masses at bay, most of the area's merchants and landowners decided to gain control of the independence armies rather than rely on Spain's undependable soldiers already battered by Napoléon. In 1821, a group of the privileged few met in Guatemala and issued a declaration of independence "to prevent the consequences to be feared in case the people themselves might proclaim it."

Nicaraguans fought hard and won the abolition of slavery in 1823. The proindependence elites then organized the Federation of Central American States, dependent on British loans for economic survival. It collapsed in 1838, when Nicaragua officially became independent.

But Nicaragua was not free. By then the British and the Americans were feasting their eyes on beautiful Lake Nicaragua as a possible site for a transisthmus canal. In 1837, U.S. millionaire Cornelius "Commodore" Vanderbilt announced his intention to build a Nicaraguan canal.

Throughout the 1850's, with U.S. government tolerance, William Walker, a 100-pound proslavery Tennessee mercenary, launched full-scale military invasions of Mexico and Central America, hoping to turn the area into a gigantic slave-labor plantation. From 1854 to 1860, Nicaraguans repeatedly fought and died to expel Walker and his fellow American mercenaries.

Natives of the Jinotega province, Nicaragua, 1931. Much of the most severe fighting between Sandino's forces and the U.S. Marines took place in this region.

In 1855, Commodore Vanderbilt finally obtained a concession to build a canal. That same year, Walker invaded Nicaragua and was "elected" president in 1856. Don Daniel warned his children never to trust the elections of the powerful.

As Nicaragua's president, Walker was granted diplomatic recognition by the U.S. government. He reinstituted slavery and made English the official language. But in a serious miscalculation, Walker cancelled Vanderbilt's canal concession. An angry Vanderbilt joined by the British financed an invasion by patriotic Nicaraguans to overthrow Walker, who escaped on an American ship. Walker returned again in 1857 to seize the port of San Juan del Norte. Once more Nicaraguan patriots, backed by the British, drove Walker out, but not for long. Three years later Walker returned via Honduras and declared himself president of Nicaragua, Honduras, and El Salvador. The British finally captured Walker and delivered him to Honduran authorities for execution by firing squad.

Nicaragua suffered several more years of dictatorship under rival elite families based in Granada and León — the Conservatives and Liberals. In 1877, Granada's Conservative government, led by Emiliano Chamorro Vargas, promulgated a law that broke up Indian communal lands and facilitated the recruitment of landless peasant laborers to harvest coffee and cut mahogany trees to sell on the world market. Naturally, the Indians and peasants rebelled, but once again resistance meant massacre: government troops killed 7,000. When the Liberal anticlerical dictatorship of President José Santos Zelaya (1893–1910) of León took over, it permitted the seizure of both church and Indian lands, allowing landowners to expand their lucrative coffee holdings even further. Like the Conservatives, the Liberal elites needed an endless supply of cheap peasant labor to support their lavish life-styles.

In 1909, when President Zelaya showed signs of allying Nicaragua with either Britain, Japan, or Germany, the United States sent in the marines to back the Conservatives, who ceded the customs revenues, railroads, and banks to the Yanquis. The new

"William Walker" in charge was U.S. Marine major general Smedley D. Butler, who later recalled "I helped purify Nicaragua for the international banking house of Brown Brothers." Augusto César Sandino was just a short, skinny 14 year old at the time of the American invasion. He was the son of a Liberal landowner and an Indian peasant woman who had been the family servant, a similar background to Don Daniel's. In 1912, the marines crushed a Liberal revolt and captured its leader, General Benjamín Zeledón and 300 of his followers, slitting the throats of some and shooting the rest. Sandino, just 17 years old and 6 inches shorter than the marines standing guard nearby, watched Zeledón's casket being taken to the cemetery. It was then that he determined to free his country from foreigners. Sandino tried to change the system by studying how it worked and by engaging in politics. However, on two issues he refused to compromise: independence for Nicaragua and a better life for the peasants.

In 1921, Sandino wounded a politician during a barroom brawl. Wanted by the police, he fled. He worked in Honduras and Guatemala and then moved to Mexico, where he found a job with a U.S. oil company in Tampico. In 1924, when he saw U.S. gunships stationed at Tampico to guarantee the interests of Standard Oil, Sandino realized again how determined the U.S. government was to protect profits. Condemning "Yankee imperialism," he wrote: "I decided . . . if there were 100 honorable men who loved their country as I did, our country's sovereignty would be restored."

Living frugally, Sandino saved money and collected contributions from his Mexican friends to finance a plan. He returned home and found his first "honorable men" among the miners of northern Nicaragua. He purchased guns and armed 29 of them. Liberal politicians added their own armed fighters, again wanting to be sure that if there was a victory, they would control it.

In 1925, thinking the situation in Nicaragua was stable for the moment, the marines withdrew. When Sandino's soldiers and the Liberal army came down

I spent most of my time being a high-class muscle man for Big Business, for Wall Street, and for the bankers. In short, I was a racketeer for capitalism.
—SMEDLEY D. BUTLER U.S. Marine general on the role of the U.S. military in Nicargua in the early 20th century

In a quest for slave labor, the diminutive Tennessee mercenary, William Walker, launched an invasion of Mexico and Central America during the 1850s. After incurring the hostility of the British, he was executed by Honduran authorities in 1860.

from the hills to close in on Managua, however, the marines returned, crushing the uprising. Sandino returned to the hills, and the marines gave chase.

In 1927, diplomat Henry L. Stimson arranged a truce with Liberal army chief José María Moncada that gave Liberals the presidency. The treaty called for disarming the Liberal and Conservative armies and creating a U.S.-trained and -armed national guard. Sandino objected: "The sovereignty and freedom of a people are not to be discussed but rather to be defended with weapons in hand."

Sandino turned down bribe offers of up to $100,000 to lay down his arms. He withdrew to Jinotega with his 300 soldiers. "It's better to die a rebel than to live as a slave," he said.

When U.S. Marine captain G. D. Hatfield ordered Sandino on July 12, 1927, to "surrender or else," Sandino responded, "Free fatherland or death." With 800 fresh recruits added to his expanding "people's army," Sandino attacked the town of Ocotal, where Captain Hatfield's marines were stationed. In one of history's first aerial bombardments, U.S. planes zoomed in low over the town, bombing and machine-gunning the fleeing civilians, leaving some 300 dead. Overwhelmed by 4,000 U.S. Marines, Sandino's forces hiked deeper into the hills. From now on, the enemy would be "the Marines of the most powerful empire in history," Sandino declared.

Most people loved Sandino, Don Daniel told his children. It was very dangerous to support Sandino's guerrillas, but many Nicaraguans provided them with food. The Ortega boys enjoyed hearing about how their father had helped Sandino. Later, Daniel Ortega told an interviewer: "Once he was taken prisoner in the mountains in the north of Nicaragua. Later, my grandfather, who was a respected director of a school in Granada, used his influence to get my father freed. . . . Well, Somoza personally scolded my father and said that the only reason he wasn't killed was my grandfather's intervention. Then Somoza gave my father a sealed envelope. When my father got home, he opened the envelope and found money inside. He immediately returned it. So Somoza responded by sending him a telegram with the following words: EAT S--T! When I was a child, my father would often show me and my brothers that telegram."

Volunteers from other Latin American countries came to join Sandino's forces and formed an international brigade. There was no way that the primitive weapons of the guerrillas could compete with the powerful arms of the invaders, but their ideals and Sandino's military strategies made a big difference. Using hit-and-run guerrilla tactics, Sandino wore the marines down. The U.S. military resorted to bombing towns, shooting prisoners, torturing detainees, and mutilating their victims' bodies. Daniel Ortega's father showed the children a picture of a smiling marine dangling severed Nicaraguan heads by the hair.

A few marines were horrified by what they were called upon to do by their commanding officers, Don Daniel hastened to point out. They deserted and joined Sandino's forces. There they discovered a band of young guerrillas called the Choir of Angels, who between battles taught the peasants of the mountainous provinces how to read. Some 20 years later those same provinces where the Choir of An-

Demonstrators protest the U.S. occupation of Nicaragua in Washington, D.C., in 1927. Lacking popular support for its interventionist policies in Central America, the United States withdrew its forces from Nicaragua in 1933, but not before setting the stage for a bloody coup and the installation of a brutal dictator.

gels had worked became a home for his comrades-in-arms and the stronghold of a revolution against Somoza III. Like Sandino, Ortega would one day be called a bandit.

In 1928, Sandino told an American reporter: "What right have foreign troops to call us outlaws and bandits and to say that we are the aggressors? I repeat that we are in our own house. We are no more bandits than was George Washington."

There were honorable American civilians who agreed with Sandino's statement and campaigned to bring the U.S. Marines home. "Hands off Nicaragua!" was their slogan, and they succeeded in pressuring Congress to vote against funds for the war. Little did Ortega realize that more than 30 years later a similar campaign would take place during his own presidency.

The marines were never able to capture or defeat Sandino. Battered and lacking popular support in the United States and in Nicaragua, they finally gave up the fight on January 1, 1933. By then, Sandino's guerrillas numbered 3,000, controlled the north, and had supporters in every major city and town.

The National Guard was turned over to General Somoza. Remaining in the presidency was Somoza's father-in-law, Juan Bautista Sacasa, who with Sandino signed a peace pact that promised land for peasant guerrillas and guaranteed Sandino's safety.

Then on February 21, 1934, came the betrayal. Somoza, shortly after conferring with American ambassador Arthur Bliss Lane, ordered guard troops to detain Sandino's party as it left a dinner at the presidential palace. Sandino and his brother were taken to a nearby airfield. There, a little after 11:00 P.M., machine-gun fire cut down Sandino, his brother, and his two leading generals. In the morning, guard troops seized the Sandinista cooperative farm at Guiguili and massacred 300 unarmed men, women, and children. In the following weeks, scores of prominent Sandinistas were executed and the movement was crushed. By 1940, some 20,000 peasants, workers, and students had fallen before the hail of guard bullets.

Soon after taking control of Nicaragua's National Guard in 1934, military strongman General Anastasio Somoza ordered the execution of several of his political rivals, including Sandino, Sandino's brother, and two leading generals. Evidence strongly suggests that the United States sanctioned the killing.

After Sandino was murdered, Somoza assured his officers that Ambassador Lane had told him the U.S. government recommended Sandino's elimination. Two years later, in 1936, Somoza took full power in a military coup by the National Guard and had himself "elected" president the following year. U.S. president Franklin D. Roosevelt said: "Somoza is an S.O.B., but he is our S.O.B."

Ortega listened attentively to the story of Sandino and his youthful band. Their dream of freedom and equality became his. Years later he told reporters that three things profoundly influenced his life: poverty, his father's stories about the invasions of the foreigners, and the betrayal of Sandino. As his parents' stories and hopes filled his head, Ortega determined that, like Sandino, he would use every possible means to place Nicaragua's vast wealth in the hands of its people.

Don Daniel Ortega and his wife, Lidia Saavedra Ortega, pose with their children — (from left) Daniel, Germana, Camilo, and Humberto. The family was poor and saw no chance of improving their lot, having made no secret of their opposition to the Somoza regime.

3

Initiation

Ortega's hatred for the regime of Somoza I deepened as he played handball on the streets of Managua, in violation of a law against loitering. National Guard trucks drove through Managua, picking up everyone who violated the law. If Daniel and his playmates ran away into side streets or alleyways, they could count on National Guardsmen chasing them with swinging clubs, throwing those they caught into the vehicles.

During World War II, despite his sympathies with dictators like Nazi Germany's Adolf Hitler and Fascist Italy's Benito Mussolini, Somoza I declared himself a U.S. ally. He seized the properties of Germans and Italians and bought the best of them at his own auctions. By the end of the war, he was the wealthiest man in the country. With Sandino dead and most of his followers exterminated, Somoza faced little active opposition. Workers demanded increased wages in 1944, and he responded with a liberal labor law. When it became clear that his reform laws would never be enforced, a few frustrated Conservatives took up arms. The guard quickly killed or arrested them in 1947.

On May 1 he (Oscar Turcios) and his friend Daniel Ortega told us what the surprise was — a huge gorilla effigy . . . representing Somoza. . . . That's a sign of repudiation used a great deal by the townspeople. Even in their religious festivities they make an effigy of Judas, hang him and then set fire to it. We used that same method to repudiate Somoza.
—DORIS TIJERINO

Chief of Staff Anastasio "Tachito" Somoza Debayle and his father, the Nicaraguan president (right), are pleased by the capture of weapons and ammunition from rebel forces in February 1955. A year later, the older Somoza was assassinated, and Tachito's brother, Luis (Somoza II), became president.

The Cuban revolutionary Fidel Castro. The Cuban revolution — in which Castro, his cohort Ernesto "Che" Guevara, and a small band of guerrilla fighters ousted the U.S.-installed dictator Fulgencio Batista — inspired young Nicaraguans who yearned for their own country's freedom from U.S. intervention.

Somoza ruled with selective cruelty. He permitted several opposition parties yet ran his own political machine and controlled Congress. Anyone who organized to achieve genuine political freedom was killed or broken in prison by the National Guard or his secret police, the Security Force.

On September 21, 1956, 11-year-old Ortega heard the good news. Worker-poet Rigoberto López pumped four bullets into Somoza as he drank and danced at a party in León. López died in a hail of bullets fired by the tyrant's bodyguards. Despite the efforts of a U.S. medical team in Panama, Somoza died a week later.

But dictatorship did not. Somoza's two sons took over: Luis Somoza became president and Anastasio "Tachito" Somoza — a 1946 graduate of the U.S. Military Academy at West Point — became chief of the National Guard.

The two brothers used their father's hard-cop, soft-cop method of governing. While Tachito used Somoza I's assassination as an excuse to arrest or imprison opposition figures, Luis announced that he would hold office for only one term and then conduct "free" elections.

Some businessmen who wanted a larger share of the economy opposed Somoza II. In an effort to appease these elites, Luis Somoza split the wealth three ways. The Somoza group kept the lion's share; the Bank of Nicaragua group, mostly Liberals, controlled cotton and commerce; and the Bank of America group, mostly Conservatives, dominated cattle ranching and trade.

It was to Somoza II's political advantage to court the upper and middle classes. Like him, they were afraid that the working people and peasants would rebel. It was reassuring for the privileged classes to know that if resistance came from any quarter, Luis's brother Tachito and the well-armed National Guard would protect them.

The landless peasants and underpaid workers continued to toil, plagued by disease and hunger. A few refused to be fooled by fake reforms and kept Sandino's torch of freedom burning. In the fall of 1958, Ramón Raudales, a veteran of Sandino's so-called people's army, heard that a small band of guerrillas in Cuba, led by Fidel Castro and Ernesto "Che" Guevara, was gaining ground against Fulgencio Batista y Zaldívar, the U.S.-installed Cuban dictator so similar to Somoza I. Raudales organized a guerrilla action in the mountains of Jalapa. He was killed by Tachito's National Guard, but others took up where he left off.

Then, on January 8, 1959, Castro and Guevara entered Havana and announced their victory to a joyous multitude. Ortega and his high school classmates were filled with renewed hope. If the Cuban guerrillas could unseat the powerful dictator Batista, Nicaraguans could get rid of the Somoza brothers.

Daniel and his friends were not the only ones who saw the parallel. Several uncoordinated guerrilla groups soon sprang up. In June, at El Chapparal near the Honduran border, one such group was ambushed by a company of the Honduran army. The National Guard closed in to finish them off. Carlos Fonseca was wounded but he managed to escape. Some day his picture would appear all over Managua as a national hero.

On July 23, 1959, university students in León protested the massacre at El Chapparal. During a peaceful march, the National Guard fired on the students from the rear, killing four of them and injuring many townspeople. Student opposition mushroomed.

Some politicians from the elite families viewed this as an opportune moment to overthrow Somoza II. One of them was Pedro Joaquín Chamorro Cardenal, son of the publisher of Nicaragua's largest newspaper, *La Prensa*. He had been among the many detained and tortured in the aftermath of Somoza I's assassination.

From Costa Rica, Chamorro put together a guerrilla band of 100 young Nicaraguans. They invaded in May 1960, but Tachito Somoza's guard proved too strong for these amateur fighters. After two weeks, they surrendered. Because they were Conservatives with only reformist goals, they were merely tried and given jail sentences instead of mas-

Pedro Joaquín Chamorro Cardenal, son of the publisher of *La Prensa*, Nicaragua's largest newspaper, and an editor himself, formed a ragtag army of fighters and led an insurrection in May 1960. His effort to oust Somoza II and institute conservative reforms failed.

sacred like the guerrillas at El Chapparal. Within a year they were free. Chamorro gave up on guerrilla warfare and returned to edit *La Prensa*. The Somoza clan often pointed to Chamorro's journalistic activities as proof that there was democracy in Nicaragua.

When none of these sporadic guerrilla actions succeeded, student supporters of both reformist and revolutionary solutions organized the Nicaraguan Patriotic Youth (JPN). Ortega was one of its early members. Ortega was a good student and worked hard for the Catholic church as well. He believed there was no contradiction between religion and overthrowing the Somozas. Several young priests avidly opposed the dictatorship. JPN members started using hit-and-run tactics against the regime, taking over a National Guard barracks in a small town for an hour or two but then leaving. Like Chamorro, they thought they could wear down the morale of the peasants who had joined the guard in order to have a job.

An apparently serious Daniel Ortega (far right) poses with some of his schoolmates. Though a good student, Ortega, first arrested for political activity in 1960, soon became less interested in his studies than in overthrowing the Somoza government.

To counter the students, Somoza's guardsmen used the same tactics they had used against handball players. They drove their trucks through Managua's streets, indiscriminately rounding up young men and women.

Ortega was arrested, beaten, and released for the first time in 1960, when he was only 15 years old. Instead of frightening him away from resistance, however, the experience appeared to strengthen his resolve.

On July 23, 1960, the JPN and other anti-Somoza groups organized demonstrations to honor the four students who had been murdered in León the previous year. A mass officiated by a sympathetic priest was planned in the chapel of Managua's General Hospital. Just as the religious ceremony started, the guard and police rushed into the hospital. They teargassed and chased students through the hospital rooms, tossing sick people out of their beds as they went. The students fled to the streets where guardsmen and police attacked wildly, turning the protest day into a full-scale riot.

University of Nicaragua students burn a U.S. flag in León in 1960 to protest U.S. support for the Somozas. Because the United States installed and actively sustained the tyrannical Somoza regime both financially and militarily for decades, anti-U.S. sentiment in Nicaragua was a natural consequence.

The climax came in the afternoon, in front of the cathedral, where an elegant wedding was in progress. Parked nearby were American Embassy limousines and the automobiles of prominent Somocistas, recognizable by their special license plates so that the police would not ticket them for speeding or parking illegally. As students marched down the street, the guard opened fire — killing a boy on crutches. Outraged, some of the students and townspeople set the parked cars ablaze.

Ortega found himself in jail again, accused of participating in the car burnings. Routinely roughed up, he remained silent.

So did the U.S. State Department. Though fully aware of the developments in Nicaragua, the U.S. government did not criticize Somoza's harsh policies. This was mainly because U.S. businessmen were investing considerable wealth in new enterprises in Central America. Some of them, especially sugar magnates, had lost plantations in Cuba when Castro's government nationalized them in order to use sugar proceeds to finance the Cuban Revolution's new hospitals, schools, and prefabricated houses. Cuba's revolutionaries believed that if one plantation owner lost his holdings and fled to his other plantations in Haiti or elsewhere, the thousands of children who could be saved from misery, poverty, and death greatly outweighed the loss.

The U.S. government did not agree. They considered it their job to defend U.S. interests abroad — which meant U.S. business interests. Some Americans felt otherwise. They protested when President Dwight Eisenhower's administration blockaded Cuba, organized terrorist activity against that country, and prohibited Americans from traveling there.

President John F. Kennedy, elected in 1960, believed that if economic aid was sent to help develop the countries of Latin America, future revolutions would be thwarted. He implemented an aid program called the Alliance for Progress. To qualify for the aid, Latin American governments would have to engage in reforms that would at least give them the appearance of having a free press and free speech, democratic elections, and provisions for giving land to hungry peasants.

Kennedy also ordered the CIA to organize and direct an invasion of Cuba by Cuban exiles, launched from Nicaragua's Atlantic coast. On April 15, 1961, Cuban exiles flying B-26 fighter planes bombed strategic military targets as well as the beach area of Bahía de Cochinos (Bay of Pigs), where the invaders, mostly supporters of the overthrown dictator Batista, landed. The CIA had assured Kennedy that the Cuban people would rise up and join the "freedom fighters." Instead, Castro proved to have much more popular support than the CIA thought. The Cuban people rushed to the beach and overwhelmed the invaders.

The Kennedy administration had no more success with the Alliance for Progress than with the Bay of Pigs invasion. The Somoza family was not about to carry out land reform or genuinely democratic elections. That would mean breaking up their own giant plantations and those of their friends and letting others run the government.

Some 300 Castro supporters demonstrate in front of the United Nations in New York on April 18, 1961. During the 1950s and 1960s, the United States was widely criticized for its interventionist policies abroad, most notably in Cuba, Central America, and Southeast Asia.

Che Guevara, the Cuban economic minister, speaks at a conference on economic and social issues on August 8, 1961, in Uruguay. Guevara, an experienced guerrilla fighter and military tactician, was an important influence on many young Nicaraguan dissidents, including Ortega.

By 1961, Ortega, just 16, began to have doubts about the JPN. The Cuban events had torn the organization apart — some supporting the socialist programs of the Cuban Revolution and others opposing them. Ortega did not know it at the time, but three young Nicaraguans were in Honduras founding the Sandinista Front of National Liberation — the FSLN. They were Carlos Fonseca, Tomás Borge, and Silvio Mayorga. All three had been involved in student politics and had been jailed, tortured, and exiled. Each one believed that because of Nicaragua's mountainous terrain, Sandino's guerrilla strategies were still the only way to mount an insurrection.

In its first appeal for recruits and aid, the FSLN announced that it intended to develop a people's army of students, peasants, and workers. Its goal was, in Fonseca's words, "the overthrow of the Somocista clique that had reduced Nicaragua to the status of neocolony" and its replacement by "a social system that wipes out exploitation and poverty."

This was Ortega's dream. After graduating from high school and entering the Jesuit-run Central American University to study law, Ortega and other students founded a branch of the FSLN's Nicaraguan Revolutionary Youth — (FER). Somoza's security agents hounded it, and Ortega left school to go underground.

In 1963, before his 18th birthday, Ortega joined the FSLN and was put in charge of the burgeoning student movement. Che Guevara's ideas on guerrilla warfare influenced young Ortega. Guevara had written that revolutionaries should gather in "wild places of small population" and promote agrarian reform. Surprise attacks from and quick retreats into these remote areas could compensate for lack of arms and training. Attacks should be limited to ambushes and disruption of communications and transport. Captured enemy soldiers should be educated, disarmed, and released. The guerrillas' objective was to survive until they were powerful enough to defeat the regular army.

The FSLN followed that advice, launching its first campaign along the Río Coco, in 1962–63 in the forested terrain of the Miskito Indian territory along the Honduran border. At a remote camp in Honduras, Fonseca and a veteran of Sandino's army, Santos López, trained a few dozen young men, most of them former students. Fonseca called for supporters in the cities to fund the operation through what he called economic "recuperations" — daring robberies of banks and businesses owned by Somocistas. Ortega answered the call. On March 3, 1963, the FSLN, in its first urban armed action, took over a radio station, Radio Mundial. It broadcast an appeal for support. The first FSLN bank robbery was carried out on May 30 at the Bank of America branch in Managua.

Ortega and his friends believed that the Somoza brothers would permit reforms only when it did not cost them anything. In June 1963, they were proven right. The first legal strike in Nicaragua in many years was repressed because it brought out large numbers of people. Earlier that year, Luis Somoza had carried out elections, allowing a limited space for free speech and promoting a puppet candidate who won.

Citizens take to the streets of Managua and hurl stones at the National Guard while others cast their ballots on February 3, 1963. The so-called election held that day was a fraud and an occasion for a flood of Somoza propaganda. Not surprisingly, Somoza II was "reelected."

Ortega and his FSLN comrades used the 1963 election as an organizing opportunity to set up committees in poor neighborhoods to pressure the government for services such as water and street lighting. Ortega proved to be a patient and successful organizer, but he became critical of the slow, patchwork reform activities. In his view, an occasional street light or new well, far from altering the basic misery of the people, sometimes raised misleading expectations that helped preserve the dictatorship.

In June 1963, the FSLN guerrilla band crossed the Río Coco from Honduras under the leadership of the elderly Santos López and 33-year-old Borge. They occupied two small villages but failed in trying to seize two others. In October, a handful of FSLN survivors retreated to Honduras, where most were captured. Two months later, Ortega was arrested in Managua and accused of planning to attack National Guard barracks. Again he was mistreated and then set free.

In early 1964, Ortega and two of his closest friends in the FER youth group, Selim Schible and Edmundo Pérez, went to Guatemala to meet with other young revolutionaries. The trio was apprehended and jailed by Guatemalan police and then turned over to Nicaraguan security agents. On the journey from Guatemala to Managua, the security men took turns savagely beating them and torturing them with lit cigarettes.

After some more beatings, Ortega was released. In 1965, he founded FER's publication *El Estudiante*, (*The Student*). He had proved himself both loyal and capable, and that year, although he was just turning 20 and was much younger than the other FSLN leaders, he was made a member of the FSLN National Directorate.

During that period, Fonseca met with Luis Turcios Lima, the leader of Guatemala's Rebel Armed Forces, the FAR. Turcios Lima admired the ideas of China's leader Mao Zedong, who had led a peasant army to victory against seemingly impossible odds in a 30-year guerrilla war. Fonseca sent a group of FSLN members to work with the FAR, gaining ex-

The Sandinista Front of National Liberation (FSLN) leadership in 1966. Back row (from left): Carlos Fonseca Amador, Roberto Amaya, Fausto Amador, and Oscar Turcios. Front row (from left): Daniel Ortega, Tomás Borge Martínez, and Rolando Rogue.

perience with what Mao had called "protracted people's war."

In the spring of 1965, when some 20,000 U.S. Marines stormed the Dominican Republic, Latin Americans were forced to admit that the reform policies of Kennedy's Alliance for Progress were fraudulent. The marines killed thousands of Dominicans in order to defeat a mass movement to reinstall their democratically elected president, reformer Juan Bosch. Once considered the darling of the Alliance for Progress, Bosch had lasted only seven months in office, overthrown by a 1963 military coup. The Dominicans had earlier ended a Somoza-style dictatorship, but the 1963 coup and 1965 invasion made it clear that the United States preferred a dictator who would keep American economic interests safe to a reformer who would allow union organizing and free speech, which might jeopardize those interests.

In January 1966, Ortega and other FSLN leaders attended the First Tricontinental Conference in Havana. They were inspired by the firsthand reports given by revolutionaries from three continents. The United States was deeply involved in Vietnam. If simultaneous guerrilla warfare were to start in several Latin American nations, there would be in Che Guevara's words, "two, three . . . many Vietnams." The Yanquis, they believed, would be so overextended that victory would be theirs.

Back in Nicaragua, the FSLN established a guerrilla camp at Pancasán, in eastern Matagalpa. Ortega took charge of urban armed operations to finance the effort. His life was totally immersed in revolutionary activity, with almost no time for recreation. Still, with his jolly, fun-loving friend Oscar Turcios, he managed to inject a little humor into the FSLN's life-risking tasks. In 1966, just before May Day — the international workers' day celebrated throughout the world — Ortega and Turcios made a little shopping excursion. They returned on May Day with a surprise present for their FSLN comrades: a big stuffed animal, a gorilla, dressed in Tachito Somoza's guard uniform with an American flag draped across its chest. At the May Day demonstration, they torched the gorilla and people laughed and danced around the burning effigy.

Ortega was also involved in efforts to convince members of the Nicaraguan Socialist party (PSN) to join the struggle. Instead, the PSN announced that it was joining the National Opposition Union (UNO), formed by the traditional Conservatives and Liberals who were running a single candidate against Tachito Somoza in the February 1967 elections. The FSLN broke off relations with the PSN in November 1966 and distributed a manifesto rejecting the elections and calling for renewed armed struggle. No organizations responded. The FSLN would be on their own. Once again, many Nicaraguans were about to be fooled by the promise of so-called free elections.

On January 20, 1967, Ortega led an FSLN squad in a robbery of a San Sebastián bank. Two days later, 60,000 people rallied in Managua to support UNO's candidate. National Guardsmen and security agents attacked the assembled crowd, killing more than 100. Many survivors of the bloody massacre found themselves agreeing with the FSLN's criticisms of "free" elections.

A month after Tachito Somoza's "election," Luis Somoza died of a heart attack. On May 1, 1967, Tachito—Somoza III—was sworn into office.

Meanwhile, hundreds of National Guard troops swarmed through Pancasán. Realizing the FSLN guerrillas there were in desperate straits, Ortega stepped up his urban insurrection campaign. On August 5, 1967, with his friend Schible, his 17-year-old brother Camilo Ortega, and several others, he robbed the safe at Managua's La Perfecta Dairy. The National Guard attacked his squad, killing Schible and taking two others prisoner, but he and the others escaped. Ortega and the FSLN vowed to take revenge on Sergeant Gonzalo Lacayo, who had tortured one of their comrades to death.

Before Ortega could even purchase arms and supplies with the stolen dairy money, National Guard reinforcements overwhelmed the Pancasán guerrillas, killing 13 of them. Guardsmen skinned 1 of the 13, Oscar Armando Flores, and left him to die as a warning to any rebellious peasants.

The few survivors fled to the cities and hid in so-called safe houses. Later, while the government scoured the cities to find the hidden Sandinistas, Borge, Humberto Ortega, and Oscar Turcios fled to Cuba, where Fonseca was waiting. On October 8, 1967, they learned that Che Guevara's luck had been even worse than their own. The Bolivian army and CIA "advisers" had captured and killed the most famous guerrilla fighter of them all. Because Guevara had gone to Bolivia to create "another Vietnam," it seemed unlikely there would be any new Vietnams.

On October 24, 1967, the FSLN carried out its first political assassination, gunning down the infamous torturer Sergeant Lacayo. The FSLN had its vengeance, but not for long. The price of such actions became clear to Ortega when the Somoza regime took its own revenge. Security agents broke into a hideout and captured four Sandinistas. Later they claimed the young fighters had died resisting, but cigarette burns and other marks of torture on their stripped bodies revealed the truth. There were protest demonstrations, followed by more arrests. Then, on November 18, 1967, the National Guard surprised Ortega and several other FSLN militants in a raid. They were accused of robbing a bank and were hauled off to prison.

The guerrillas were gone from Pancasán, and the urban section of the FSLN was now silent. Tachito Somoza proclaimed that the Sandinistas no longer existed. Ortega sat in jail, about to suffer his worst tortures yet.

4

In and Out of the Enemy's Hands

When the National Guardsmen threw Ortega in jail this time, they intended to force him to reveal the names of everyone involved in the FSLN urban work. They tried to break him, but he preferred death to betrayal and would not talk. For years, Ortega found it impossible to give details of those terrible seven years. It was not until the 1980s, when the memories had dulled, that he began to speak of them. Even then, he played down the horrors, but journalists pieced them together from graphically violent poems he wrote in jail.

When an interviewer asked Ortega if he really believed that Somoza's jails were comparable to the Nazi concentration camps, Ortega described his ordeal in the Managua prison: "I was in a tiny cell with 150 other prisoners. . . . We had only one toilet. . . . You got one tortilla, a small one, and maybe 30 beans — you could count them. . . . There was a code among the common criminals to respect the political prisoners, but sometimes, when the prison warden came to visit, the common criminals were ordered to beat us. Later, they'd excuse themselves.

There were six concentration camps set up in the north. In April 1976 over a hundred families disappeared from three hamlets. Their bodies were never found. Altogether, some 3,000 deaths are estimated to have occurred during the three years of the state of siege.
—ALISON ROOPER
American writer

Ortega is arrested and escorted to prison by one of Somoza's National Guardsmen in 1967. He spent the next seven years in jail — where he was poorly fed, blindfolded, and tortured by prison guards — but even from his cell he remained politically active.

Needless to say, there was torture — and a lot of isolation periods. Beatings—many beatings."

Ortega would bear a scar on his temple for the rest of his life. In the first weeks after his arrest, Ortega was beaten repeatedly, suffering several broken ribs. Then his torturers went for his face, almost blinding him. Close to death, Ortega huddled in a cage — alone, naked, and starved, unable to see because of a cloth bag covering his head.

The only way to stay alive was to publicize the plight of the prisoners. With his quiet sincerity, Ortega excelled at persuading some of the young and ignorant prison guards to carry messages to the outside. In this way, he was able to convert his trial into a political event, with supporters stirring up international publicity on the unspeakable tortures, including the sexual humiliation and rape of incarcerated women. Several commanders of the FSLN were women, including two arrested with Ortega — Gladys Baez and Doris Tijerino.

From his cell, Ortega directed mothers' strikes on the outside and hunger strikes by prisoners on the inside, one lasting 42 days. He seemed to be able to bring people together, to lead quietly, to endure without complaint. With the help of a few willing guards, he and his comrades planned some escape attempts, but none succeeded. Somoza's henchmen tortured Ortega every time a new escape plan was suspected or an anti-Somoza action took place outside.

During periods when he was left alone, Ortega did many things to keep his spirit from crumbling. He studied, exercised regularly, and engaged in the Nicaraguans' most popular pastime after baseball — poetry. To his surprise, his poems were published in literary magazines and even read aloud in public.

It must have seemed to Ortega that he would remain in prison forever. In September 1968, almost a year after his arrest, another large group of urban commandos joined him in prison. It was obvious that the FSLN was losing and had to reassess its approach. Accordingly, Sandinista exiles met in Costa Rica and adopted the Prolonged Popular War strategy, deciding to organize more support among the people and to risk fewer of their precious cadres in commando operations. They restricted FSLN membership to only 50 persons — those tested over a long period.

When things looked hopeless, support for the struggle came from an unexpected quarter — the Catholic church. A 1963 conference of Latin American bishops in Medellín, Colombia, called for a radical redistribution of wealth in all Latin America and blamed the rich industrialized nations for much of the area's economic misery. Just as the U.S. government had issued its Alliance for Progress in an effort to stem the tide of revolution after Castro's victory in Cuba, so the Catholic church was trying to win back millions of young Latin Americans inspired by the Cuban Revolution.

Regardless of the bishops' motivations, their Medellín declaration had a profound impact. Seven Nicaraguan priests publicly called for an end to torture, political imprisonment, and the wide gap between rich and poor. Many Catholics began to feel that they could now support the FSLN without offending the church. Priests began translating their "liberation theology" into action, organizing peasants into Christian Base Communities and Agricultural Workers Committees.

Tachito Somoza, his wife, Hope, and numerous Somocistas enjoy an elaborate luncheon at the Airforce Club in Managua in 1967. His wife left him in the 1970s, when Somoza developed a romantic interest in a prostitute, Dinorah Sampson, to whom he gave a chain of fancy boutiques.

In 1969, the FSLN's National Directorate published its program appealing to all segments of the population. It promised jobs and the right to organize for workers; equality and day-care centers for women; cooperative farms instead of private plantations; participation in government for everyone; crop diversification to provide enough food for all; freedom of speech; health care; quality education; literacy programs; religious freedom; and, best yet, replacement of the National Guard with a people's army and a civilian militia. At the same time, the FSLN suspended large-scale guerrilla operations.

Still, from the late 1960s to the mid-1970s, the Somoza regime maintained the upper hand. In searching for guerrilla sympathizers, National Guard troops burned entire villages down, advised by the same U.S. military men who had become experts at such maneuvers during the Vietnam War. Each time the guard withdrew, it left battered bodies of peasants and their families strewn over the countryside. An occasional bank robbery or assassination of a particularly brutal National Guard officer led to further beatings of prisoners like Ortega.

The Costa Rican government gave in to the pressures of the Somoza regime and the U.S. Embassy and clamped down on the activities of FSLN exiles in their country. In June 1969, it deported Oscar Turcios to Spain. In September, Ortega's spirits further slumped when he learned that Fonseca had been captured during a bank robbery in Costa Rica. The FSLN hijacked an airliner to pressure for Fonseca's freedom, but the Costa Rican authorities refused to release their star prisoner. The repercussions from the Americans and Somoza would have been too great.

Right before Christmas, Ortega received more demoralizing news. His brother Humberto had been wounded and captured during an attack on the Alejuela jail in Costa Rica, where Fonseca languished behind bars. Humberto Ortega never regained the use of his right arm.

In 1970, a few rays of hope glimmered through the bleakness. Daniel Ortega learned that the FER

Number one, the Sandinista terrorists had a hard-core group of leftist priests. . . . Number two, the rebel movement was without men and money. . . . Number three, the women among the terrorists who held the hostages were far more vicious than the men.

—ANASTASIO SOMOZA
on the December 1974
Christmas Raid negotiations

had won elections at the national university. Then Miguel Obando y Bravo became archbishop of Managua and began to criticize the Somoza regime. Meanwhile, in Chile, a democratic socialist, Salvador Allende, actually won the presidential election. But in terms of FSLN actions, the news remained very bad.

On May Day 1970, the National Guard broke up student-worker demonstrations. In response, students joined with the mothers of political prisoners and staged hunger strikes in and out of the prisons that lasted through July. Ortega coordinated the actions from jail.

In September, university students occupied the National Cathedral and held another hunger strike calling for the freedom of political prisoners. The Liberal party split when a large sector called for an end to Somoza's rule. Every little bit of good news helped the prisoners bear up under their oppressive conditions. Ortega's steadying presence prevented many of them from giving in to torture and demoralization.

On October 21, 1970, the prisoners celebrated when they heard about another hijacking of a Costa Rican plane. This time four American United Fruit officials were held hostage. With such a privileged cargo, the FSLN finally won freedom for Fonseca, as well as for Humberto Ortega and several others.

In November, Tachito Somoza, confident that serious challenges to his regime no longer existed, granted Conservative politicians some seats in Congress and representation on a powerless Executive Triumvirate. *La Prensa* editor Chamorro opposed the fraudulent "democratization," and his party expelled him. He promptly organized the Conservative National Action (ANC), recruiting a small but growing number of businesspeople and professionals who no longer felt tolerant toward Somoza III.

By the end of 1970, 17 FSLN leaders were in captivity, leaving Oscar Turcios, who had sneaked back from Spain, as the only free National Directorate member inside Nicaragua. Several more Sandinistas slipped in from exile to fill the leadership gap, most of them going to the mountains to attempt to

All the prisoners joined in the hunger strikes we carried out in prison so we could be set free. The mothers too; our mothers, the mothers of the condemned comrades, sisters, representatives of political organizations, and of the student movement. The struggle for the freeing of the prisoners and the solidarity and support for the prisoners was a struggle headed by women.
—DORIS TIJERINO

President Salvador Allende shares his views on Chile's housing crisis in 1970. Allende's economic reforms, which entailed the nationalization of many U.S. industries in Chile, angered U.S. president Richard Nixon, who promptly acted to oust the Chilean leader. The result: Allende's assassination, the death of some 30,000 Allende supporters, and the installation of a brutal military dictatorship.

rebuild the guerrilla groups. With Managua controlled by the National Guard, urban organizing focused on León, under the command of Turcios.

Many people believed that aside from the poor men and women trapped in prison, Somoza had told the truth when he claimed the FSLN had been destroyed. Consequently, the activities of students and church people became more important. In April 1971, they, along with Ortega and other prisoners, organized a nationwide occupation of churches and schools that won the release of several prisoners — but not Ortega.

In May, the church hierarchy, led by Obando y Bravo, condemned the violence of the Somoza regime. Young Catholic radical priests took the hierarchy for its word and formed the Christian Revolutionary Movement (MCR). They organized at universities and in city slums.

Managua was devastated by the 1972 earthquake: Thousands were killed, and 90 percent of the city's population were rendered homeless by the disaster. Remarkably, a cathedral remains standing amid piles of the rubble.

Until the earthquake on December 23, 1972, frequent hunger strikes and student demonstrations seemed futile to many activists. Somoza allowed window-dressing congressional elections in February 1972, and seemed even more secure in June when the Central American Defense Council (CONDECA), armed and trained by the United States, held joint military exercises. The training of new recruits included participation in a massacre of FSLN supporters at El Crucero.

In December, the American millionaire Howard Hughes arrived in Managua, planning to invest in joint casino enterprises with the Somoza regime. Having been forced out of their casino, prostitution, and drug-running enterprises in Havana by the Cuban Revolution, several businesspeople had come to Nicaragua. The word was out that opposition had been destroyed. Whatever remained — unarmed stu-

Santa guzzles an icy Coca-Cola while a displaced Managua family tries to cope in the aftermath of the Nicaraguan earthquake on December 23, 1972. Central America's political and economic ills, so often blamed on policies of the wealthy industrialized nations of the world, were compounded by the damage caused by the quake.

dents, mothers, a few priests and their followers — presented no problem, just an annoyance. Investments in Nicaraguan enterprises could not be more secure. Jolted awake in the Hotel Intercontinental when the earthquake hit on December 23, Hughes left on the first plane out.

Somoza's greedy behavior after the earthquake shifted the balance of power. From the point of view of business investors, it was one thing to divert relief aid and make land and construction deals that swelled one man's wealth while the majority of the country's population went hungry; it was quite another thing, however, to cut them out of the advantageous investment opportunities. Audible mumblings of discontent were heard.

In 1973, FSLN leaders sadly pointed to another lesson in the futility of elections as long as armies remained loyal to the forces of reaction. The Chilean military overthrew the democratically elected government of Salvador Allende and killed 30,000 Allende supporters.

The FSLN still avoided direct confrontation with the National Guard, concentrating on building support among homeless refugees of the earthquake, trade unionists, and radicalized Christians. Their patient work bore fruit when the priest-led MCR agreed that only armed struggle could end Somoza's iron rule. They officially joined with the FSLN as an "intermediate organization."

Throughout the rest of 1973 and all of 1974, activities against the dictatorship accelerated. The FSLN participated in many of them, from peasant land takeovers to student-led protests against bus fare increases. As Somoza grew worried over the mounting opposition, the National Guard stepped up its grisly activities.

In September 1973, during his seventh year in jail, Ortega learned that his old friend Oscar Turcios had fallen into the hands of Somoza's gorillas, who were much more lethal than the stuffed gorilla they had laughed over in 1966. Joking, fun-loving Oscar Turcios was sliced up and killed. In the next day or two, three more anti-Somoza militants died. FSLN leaders quarreled over whether urban operations should be suspended.

In January 1974, FSLN leaders decided to renew guerrilla operations, first creating a dependable underground supply line from the León area to Jinotega. Some FER and MCR youths agreed to join the guerrilla squads. In March, several businessmen, still angry over Somoza's extortion of the earthquake profits, decided to oppose Somoza's upcoming September bid for a second presidential term.

In May, women who had never been active before joined the opposition ranks when they heard about Amanda Piñeda's testimony. Piñeda, a peasant mother of nine, told a horrifying story of the National Guard repeatedly raping her and threatening to drop her from a helicopter, then beating and burning her friends in front of her and half burying them in ant hills. Her husband, exiled abroad, rushed home only to be seized by the guard.

In June 1974, Chamorro called for a boycott of the elections. Several weeks later, the Bishops' Conference openly challenged the morality of a Liberal-

Oscar had a very jovial character. He was always singing and cracking jokes. He was a very generous person; it didn't matter to him if he sacrificed his well-being to help others.
—DORIS TIJERINO

General Tachito Somoza (Somoza III), who became president of Nicaragua on May 1, 1967, after his brother, Luis (Somoza II), died of a heart attack, presides over an earthquake emergency committee meeting in 1973. Somoza used most of the earthquake relief aid sent by other nations to Nicaragua to line his already stuffed pockets.

Conservative pact that virtually assured Somoza's reelection. In November, Chamorro called for unity among Christian Democrats, trade unionists, businesspeople, and even the Communist PSN, inviting them all to join his Democratic Union of Liberation (UDEL).

On the evening of December 27, 1974, the FSLN carried out its most daring operation to date. A post–Christmas Day party in honor of American ambassador Turner Shelton was in progress in the fancy Los Robles neighborhood of Managua at the home of José María "Chema" Castillo Quant, a close friend of Tachito Somoza. The house echoed with the sounds of laughing, drinking guests, mostly diplomats and government bigwigs. Suddenly, only minutes after Ambassador Shelton's departure, 10 men and 3 women, the "Juan José Quezada" commando, burst into the house and took the guests hostage at gunpoint. The commandos shot Castillo when he resisted.

With Archbishop Obando y Bravo heading up the negotiations, Somoza III agreed to release 14 political prisoners and fly them to Cuba along with their liberators. He would pay $2 million out of the $5 million demanded by the rebels, raise the minimum wage, and publicize an FSLN message in the press and on television. Within a few days, immense crowds were lining the Managua airport roads to cheer Ortega and 13 other prisoners along their route to freedom. As Somoza's agreement stipulated, Archbishop Obando y Bravo flew with them to Cuba.

Ortega's mother had often told her sons that Obando y Bravo had been raised in their hometown. Don Daniel and his wife had known the archbishop's parents. On the plane to Cuba, Ortega chatted with Obando y Bravo, later telling author Salman Rushdie that the archbishop seemed "very frightened. I asked him what was the matter and he finally said, 'Do you think Somoza put a bomb on the plane?' " After Ortega assured him the FSLN had checked the plane, Obando y Bravo asked, "Do you think they will arrest me when we land in Cuba?" Ortega replied, "Do you seriously think Fidel is going to put you in jail?" The archbishop's thinking struck Ortega as provincial.

A young commando journeyed to Cuba on the same aircraft. Her name was Comandante Leticia Herrera. Soon she would fall in love with one of the men she helped to free—Daniel Ortega.

After seven years of torture and near starvation in a Somoza prison, Ortega was released and flown to Cuba. Immediately he plunged himself into political activity. He was a man with an obsession: Somoza had to be beaten.

5

The Long Road to Victory

After seven years of imprisonment, it seemed unreal," Ortega commented to an interviewer about his stay of several months in Cuba. "It took all of us quite a while to adapt ourselves to freedom." But adapt he did, improving his health and touring the island. He visited schools, housing projects, health stations, cooperative farms, and received some military training.

One day in Havana, Ortega recognized Rosario Murillo leaving a museum. They had grown up in the same town but had never met. As Murillo approached Ortega, she also recognized him from his newspaper photographs. They chatted for a while and parted, not realizing that years later they would be Nicaragua's "first family." Only 23 years old, Murillo had achieved fame as a poet. She and Ortega had similar dreams and memories — a future Nicaraguan revolution and childhood stories of Sandino.

The silhouette was familiar. Sandino's figure, complete with ten-gallon hat and breeches, peers out from the walls of countless buildings in Nicaragua.
—ALISON ROOPER
American writer

A masked Sandinista guerrilla fighter in León in 1979. A hotbed of opposition to the Somoza regime since the 1930s, León was never entirely subdued by the National Guard. The city was the site of the assassination of Somoza I in 1956.

Murillo, in fact, was Sandino's grandniece. After her grandmother died in childbirth, Sandino's parents raised her mother. The day of Sandino's murder, his parents had decorated their house for the first communion date of Murillo's mother. Later her mother showed her an envelope with a strand of Sandino's blood-caked hair. Murillo inherited the last clothes that Sandino wore before he changed into his fancier outfit to keep his fatal dinner date at the presidential palace.

Ortega longed to get back into action again, especially when hearing that Somoza had used the Christmas party raid as a pretext for a vicious clampdown. Nicaragua was living under martial law, and the guard was burning mountain towns and herding peasants into resettlement camps.

Somoza's crackdown plunged Ortega into renewed FSLN debates. Two "tendencies" emerged, but they were more like divisions. One, championed by Jaime Wheelock, son of a wealthy landowner and restaurateur, became known as the "Proletarian Tendency." It called for focusing on organizing urban workers and rural wage laborers. The second tendency, championed by Borge, advocated rural guerrilla warfare — the Prolonged People's War strategy. Fonseca, the FSLN's most respected leader, returned to Managua to try to heal the rupture but failed.

In February 1976, the National Guard captured Borge in Managua and threw him into solitary confinement. On November 8, while on guerrilla patrol near Jinotega, Fonseca fell before a hail of guard bullets. Between December and January, some 3,000 Salvadoran and Guatemalan soldiers joined National Guard and U.S. Ranger units in Operation Aguila Z, wiping out all but a few of the remaining FSLN guerrillas. When a jubilant Somoza received Fonseca's head, he again announced that the Sandinistas no longer existed.

Ortega began to have doubts about the Prolonged People's War strategy. His brother Humberto joined him on the FSLN National Directorate, and they put forward a third tendency, the *Tercerista* (third) or Insurrectional Tendency. The Ortegas argued that

> *We began to receive reports that there was trouble in some of the high schools. Students bent on disorder would intercept other students and threaten them if they attended class. If that didn't work, the problem students would go to class themselves and attempt to disrupt the routine. On the part of the students, this was a form of protest against the government.*
>
> —ANASTASIO SOMOZA

popular discontent with Somoza would boil over, making conditions ripe for an insurrection to topple him. But victory would be achieved only if alliances were built between the FSLN and other anti-Somoza forces, even conservative businesspeople. Ortega noted that president-elect Jimmy Carter had spoken out on human rights violations, which meant that the Americans would at least not interfere as boldly as they had in the past. Moreover, Nicaragua's bishops had protested Somoza's murder of the mountain peasants, and priests were organizing opposition to Somoza. An attempt must be made, he insisted, to unite all of the anti-Somoza forces regardless of their ideology.

In 1977, Ortega's predictions came true. As news of ongoing peasant massacres spread, protest meetings erupted throughout the nation. In March, Carter's State Department made its first public criticism of Somoza's human rights record, and the U.S. Congress began debating a bill to halt military aid to Somoza. In the summer, students disrupted public transportation to protest bus fare hikes, and Carter suspended payment on military credits.

Ortega, who was in charge of the internal front, traveled secretly to Managua and nearby Masaya to set up plans for a popular insurrection. Meanwhile, his brother Humberto Ortega met with Sergio Ramírez — a famous Nicaraguan writer living in Costa Rica and a secret member of the FSLN — and eight prominent Nicaraguans recruited by Ramírez. Their discussions led to the founding of the "Group of Twelve," an underground body composed of Catholic priests, a lawyer, a banker, a supermarket chain owner, and several professionals. If an FSLN offensive scheduled for October succeeded, the Group of Twelve would form a provisional government.

In September, under pressure from President Carter, Somoza ended martial law. Ortega assumed command of the Carlos Fonseca Northern Front and began preparing for attacks on several guard headquarters. The October offensive, however, did not touch off a full-scale insurrection. Somoza used it to convince President Carter to restore U.S. military aid.

To evaluate human rights properly, Mr. Carter doesn't have to go to Nicaragua, Chile, or Argentina. What about human rights violations in the United States? To observe gross human rights violations, all one has to do is visit any Indian reservation in the United States.
—ANASTASIO SOMOZA responding to President Carter's charges of human rights violations by the Nicaraguan government

In the course of fighting together against the guard and camping in the mountains, Ortega and Leticia Herrera became lovers. Herrera, five years Ortega's junior, was the daughter of a Nicaraguan man who had fled Somoza's repression. She had been raised in Costa Rica by her Costa Rican mother. Selected to participate in the 1974 Christmas party raid because of her courage, she was called Miriam during her guerrilla years. Herrera had a young son, left in the care of his grandmother. In 1978, she gave birth to Ortega's first son, Camilo. In 1979, Herrera told an interviewer, "Work has always separated couples, and sometimes the separation is permanent. Here we value work over personal life."

Ortega's progress toward uniting all those opposed to Somoza received a big boost from a tragic event in early 1978: the assassination of *La Prensa* editor Pedro Joaquín Chamorro. Chamorro had taken advantage of Somoza's eased censorship to publicize a scandal taking place inside three white buildings in Managua known as La Casa de Vampiros — the House of Vampires. There, inside many sterile rooms, the city's poor came to "earn" a little money by bleeding into plastic bags. Donors were paid about $5 per unit and each was sold for $50.

Some 100,000 mourners surround the coffin of the newspaper editor Pedro Joaquín Chamorro Cardenal, a longtime Somoza critic, who was gunned down on his way to work on January 10, 1978. Somoza and the "blood merchant" Pedros Ramos were allegedly responsible for the murder.

Every month, 20,000 liters of plasma were shipped to the United States. Many of Managua's unemployed returned over and over again to La Casa de Vampiros, their only source of income. La Casa's annual take was more than $12 million. Dr. Pedros Ramos, who had fled from Cuba to continue his wretched activities in Somoza's safe house, became a multimillionaire from his blood profits.

What few realized, until Chamorro exposed the secret in *La Prensa*, was that Ramos was not the only bloodsucker enriching himself. His partner was none other than Tachito Somoza. Ramos sued Chamorro for libel and lost his case.

On the way to his office on January 10, 1978, Chamorro was gunned down on the street. The gunman was quickly captured and revealed that he had been hired by Ramos. But the doctor was not available for questioning. He was far away in Miami, where it was difficult to extradite him, Tachito Somoza explained through his American press secretary Norman Wolfson.

Blaming Somoza for Chamorro's assassination, 100,000 incensed Nicaraguans joined a funeral march in Managua's streets. Chamorro's UDEL called a successful general strike and demanded Somoza's resignation. People who for years had scampered by Managua's three white buildings averting their eyes now set La Casa de Vampiros ablaze. Thousands demonstrated in Masaya and León waving Sandinista red-and-black flags. Somoza declared a state of emergency and attacked public gatherings. Each new guard assault on people suspected of being muchachos provoked additional insurrectional activity by Nicaragua's youth.

Acts of solidarity poured in from abroad. Venezuelan unions cut all oil exports to Somoza's Nicaragua. Newspapers around the world called the Somoza regime a brutal dictatorship.

In early February 1978, the Terceristas launched yet another offensive. Ortega, his brother Camilo, and Edén Pastora attacked National Guard barracks in different parts of the country. The long-isolated guerrillas in the northeastern mountains also resumed their attacks.

Chamorro must have been bitter because he didn't have a piece of the plasma plant which Ramos ran. . . . After Chamorro was killed . . . the agitators decided they wanted to kill all the foreigners and Cubans who worked in the blood bank. There wasn't much logic to their thinking but, then, what mob has any logic at all?
—ANASTASIO SOMOZA

FSLN guerrilla leader Edén Pastora, "Comandante Cero," boards a plane bound for Panama. In exchange for the release of more than 1,000 congressmen and government workers he had held hostage, Pastora took $500,000 from Somoza's coffers to help finance FSLN activities and 58 Sandinistas whom Somoza had jailed.

revoking the Chamber of Commerce charter and arresting 200 business leaders. His response to U.S. State Department criticisms was to have a spokesman label its Human Rights Bureau "Marxist."

With additional arms from the governments of Venezuela and Costa Rica, Ortega's FSLN Terceristas launched a new offensive on September 9, 1978. Ortega himself took charge of the southern front and coordinated attacks on National Guard posts in all major cities, including Managua. Despite reservations, the other two FSLN tendencies participated, and scores of poorly armed civilians joined in the fighting. Elite troops were sent in to reinforce guard garrisons, retaking the cities one by one at great cost of life.

On October 6, the U.S. State Department's William Bowdler arrived in Nicaragua to propose a national plebiscite. Somoza countered with an offer to "power-share." But the Nicaraguan people, now beyond that point, paid little attention to the meetings. Six of the Group of Twelve withdrew from the negotiations in protest and took refuge from the National Guard in the Mexican Embassy.

On December 4, 1978, Ortega achieved what he had patiently worked for since June: a unified command of the three FSLN tendencies. Popular with all three factions, Ortega played a leading role in healing the breach. There were rumors that Fidel Castro had urged the reconciliation by threatening to withdraw Cuban aid.

As Christmas drew near, U.S. officials attempted to convince Somoza to step down. It took seven more months of death and destruction before Somoza finally agreed. In February 1979, the U.S. government cancelled its military agreements with Somoza, suspended economic aid, and recalled half its embassy staff.

On Easter Sunday, Tercerista Francisco Rivera led 200 fighters into Estelí and held the city for over a week despite a ruthless bombardment. But every time it seemed that Somoza would finally resign, more money flowed to him. On May 14, 1979, the International Monetary Fund gave Somoza a $66 million loan to shore up his battle for continued power.

The final FSLN offensive lasted from late May until the middle of July 1979. Ortega's tactic of unabated attacks was wearing down the National Guard. On June 3, nearly 230 FSLN fighters led by Leticia Herrera, Dora María Tellez, and others surrounded León's 600-strong National Guard garrison. They kept it tied down for several weeks, while a general strike called by the FSLN and FAO paralyzed the entire nation. On June 6, the FSLN led another insurrection in Masaya, followed three days later by one in Estelí. Guardsmen fled in disarray toward Managua, itself in desperate need of reinforcements.

The Battle of Managua lasted from June 9 to June 27. As fighting spread throughout the capital city, Somoza ordered an increase in saturation bombings. In the south, Ortega and Edén Pastora took Peñas Blancas in a surprise attack. Trench warfare along the Pan-American Highway prevented supplies from getting through to National Guard units in the capital.

On December 4, 1978, Ortega achieved a unified command of the three FSLN factions. Here several leaders gather to announce the unity agreement (from left): Jaime Wheelock, Daniel Ortega, Tomás Borge, Henry Ruiz, Victor Tirado, and Humberto Ortega.

On June 16, Ortega became a member of the newly named five-person Junta of National Reconstruction that included Chamorro's widow, Violeta Chamorro, and the wealthy Robelo. U.S. negotiators pressed for an even more moderate government in exchange for Somoza's resignation.

But the FSLN leaders held all the cards at the negotiating table. Their courage and the determination of the Nicaraguan people had already sealed Somoza's fate. On June 21, the U.S. government vainly tried to get the Organization of American States (OAS) to approve a multinational military force to go into Nicaragua "to restore order." The OAS instead passed a resolution calling for an end to arms shipments to all factions, Somoza's replacement by a transitional government (the Junta), and early free elections. By then, even Somoza knew the end had come.

A street scene in Estelí, Nicaragua, September 1978. Barricades constructed by Sandinista rebel forces and local citizens represent the people's concerted effort to resist the National Guard's fascist aggression and pave the way for democracy and socialism.

On July 7, the major National Guard fortress in León fell to forces under the command of Leticia Herrera. Three days later, Ortega and Tomás Borge entered "the free territory of León" to a hero's welcome. They waved their red-and-black scarves to the cheering throngs. On July 16, the decisive victory of Estelí occurred. Somoza resigned the next day.

On July 19, Ortega rode into a bombed-out Managua to a second resounding welcome. Later he commented on those final days: "The triumph in Managua was kind of anticlimactic for me. . . . We had already captured León, and Somoza had fled. . . . There we were, resting up for the next day's march, watching television in León. And on that night, for the first time, I saw some old film footage of Sandino being broadcast. During all the years of Somoza, we had never seen any film of him and I had known about Sandino only from photographs and books. But there he actually was, waving his hat! And *that* was the thing that impressed me most, to see Sandino waving his hat on TV."

National Guardsmen armed with machine guns and heavy artillery patrol the streets of Masaya, Nicaragua, in June 1979. The guardsmen terrorized the town briefly before moving on to Managua, where the fighting was most intense.

6

In Power

As Ortega surveyed the cheering throngs at the Junta's inauguration on July 20, 1979, he knew he faced formidable tasks. Somoza's bombs and machine guns had killed or wounded six percent of the population. More than a million people were homeless, unemployed, orphaned, roaming the rubble-filled cities and towns. Two out of three peasants had no land. During the final offensive, crops went unplanted, industry was destroyed. Where would the food be found to feed the hungry? How would the Junta find the money to rebuild industry?

The country's health problems were staggering, too. Thousands of deaths resulted from polluted water. Disease was rampant, and the average life expectancy for Nicaraguans was 53. Trained personnel and medical facilities were desperately needed.

In the Sandinista revolution there is no alignment; there is an absolute and consistent commitment to the aspirations of the peoples who have achieved their independence and to those who are struggling to win it. That is why we are among the Nonaligned.
—DANIEL ORTEGA
address to Havana Summit
Meeting of Nonaligned
Nations, September 1979

Daniel Ortega, head of Nicaragua's provisional government, addresses a crowd of cheering supporters in Managua on July 19, 1979. The task before the new government would not be easy: Nearly half a century of extortion and exploitation by the Somoza regime left Nicaragua with staggering economic and social problems.

Four members of the Sandinista junta (starting third from left) — Daniel Ortega, Sergio Ramírez, Violeta Chamorro (wife of Pedro Joaquín Chamorro), and Alfonso Robelo — are flanked by high-ranking officers of the rebel movement soon after taking power in July 1979.

Millions of dollars were required to turn things around. But Somoza and his cronies had deposited nearly half a billion dollars, much of it borrowed, in bank accounts abroad. Now Nicaragua was burdened by Somoza's foreign debt. Export earnings could never pay it off because U.S. investors, through their dominant influence over banking and trade, ended up pocketing a lion's share of export profits. Some Sandinistas suggested cancellation of the foreign debt. But others, including Ortega, feared such an action would bring reprisals.

Reluctantly, the Junta announced it would pay all the country's creditors except two: Israel and Argentina. "We will not pay one cent of it," Ortega said of those debts, because both nations had financed arms for the National Guard when Carter had cut off U.S. military aid. In the national treasury Junta members found only $3.5 million. Somoza had sacked that too.

In September 1979, the Junta sent Ortega abroad to seek economic assistance. Ortega was the logical choice. Not the most dynamic speaker or the most ideologically inclined of the Junta members, he was respected by both conservatives and leftists as a patient and clever strategist. A flexible man, he genuinely believed in political pluralism and a mixed economy of both state-owned and private properties, and he could be counted on to control his temper.

Ortega's first stop was the Havana summit meeting of the Nonaligned Nations. "We know that U.S. imperialism is interested in seeing our process fail," he told the assembled delegates. Then he journeyed to Washington.

American politicians expected an unsmiling, difficult young man. They reportedly expressed surprise at his easy manner when he met with President Carter. At the United Nations, Ortega again pleaded for international aid.

In late November, a U.S. aid package of $75 million was finally approved. Ortega's diplomacy had worked. But in less than two months Carter cut off the aid based on what later turned out to be a false claim that the Nicaraguans were sending arms to rebels fighting the U.S.-supported dictatorship in El Salvador.

All told, Nicaragua obtained $580 million — not enough to pay even the interest on the national debt, but better than nothing. Still, the nation could not survive forever on borrowed money. The income from flourishing farms and businesses would have to be the answer. The first step was to nationalize Somoza's vast farmlands and business properties. Income from the new state property would be used for the common good, instead of for the high living of a privileged few. Banking and foreign trade, insurance, transportation, mining and forestry, and

Ortega and other Nicaraguan delegates meet with President Jimmy Carter (opposite Ortega), Vice-president Walter Mondale (seated, far left), and other U.S. representatives in late 1979. Following the meeting, Carter offered the junta a $75-million aid package for Nicaragua, but the offer was later withdrawn.

most of the construction industry were also nationalized. Leaving half of industry and the rest of commercial agriculture in private hands, the government paid compensation to all former non-Somocista owners.

Most Nicaraguans welcomed these socialist measures. But the government's next announcement angered them. In honoring earlier agreements with U.S. negotiators for no reprisals against the National Guard, the Junta called for an end to executions of known guard torturers and murderers. It abolished the death penalty, decreed a maximum jail sentence of 30 years, and released hundreds of captured guardsmen from jail. The Nicaraguan people, as Alan Riding reported in the *New York Times*, were infuriated. One mother whose three sons had been killed by one of the freed guardsmen complained that he was already threatening her. Other victims' mothers stormed the Sandinista military command in León, decrying the Junta's policy. In September 1980, a bomb was placed by Argentine guerrillas in Tachito Samoza's Mercedes-Benz, blowing him to bits. Nicaraguans responded with a fiesta in the streets.

Perhaps Ortega and his comrades regretted their decision later when the U.S.-financed former guardsmen — called contras, short for counterrevolutionaries — plunged the nation into a devastating war. The contras blew up oil refineries, poisoned water wells, and targeted the symbols of revolutionary progress, destroying schools, hospitals, and health centers, and kidnapping and murdering hundreds of teachers and health workers.

Clearly, the revolution had to defend itself with, in Sandino's words, "weapons in hand." Ortega's brother Humberto took charge of a new Sandinista People's Army, one that in a few years grew to 50,000.

In charge of the government's day-to-day operations, Daniel Ortega worked 20 hours a day. But he was not too busy for romance when Rosario Murillo became his assistant. In the intervening years since they had met outside a Havana museum in 1974, Murillo had married an FSLN militant and given birth to two children before the National Guard captured and killed her husband. She worked at *La Prensa* with Chamorro until his assassination in 1978. That year she joined the team of Radio Sandinista, the FSLN clandestine radio station. She was often detained and roughed up by Somoza's security agents. While working together, Ortega and Murillo fell in love. Their home and family would be a peaceful oasis during the trying times ahead.

After his trip abroad, another problem weighed on Ortega's mind. The FSLN program promised to build Nicaragua's first democracy based on political pluralism, a mixed economy, and nonalignment in foreign policy. Would the United States allow all that? Had it allowed Sandino's similar program to be realized? Ortega still recalled his father's stories of Sandino's betrayal and the several decades of the U.S.-trained guards riding roughshod over the people. He publicly warned that if American soldiers touched one inch of Nicaraguan territory the people would resist, and many Americans would come home in body bags, just as they had from Vietnam.

To avoid such a bloody scenario, Ortega thought it necessary to maintain the fragile unity with the business sector. Some of Ortega's FSLN comrades, such as Interior Minister Tomás Borge, argued for fewer concessions. At a meeting of 31 FSLN commanders, Ortega's pragmatic approach won out. Left-wing agitators would be controlled and business interests reassured.

Many people were disappointed. In the first few months of the revolution in power, the word *socialism* filled the air. Even the Catholic church, in its first post-Somoza pastoral letter, advocated "true socialism."

But Ortega knew better. Nicaragua's capitalists and the Church hierarchy would never accept socialism. Even with a mixed economy, how long would they cooperate with the Sandinistas? Would they go along with government-sponsored redistribution of land and income, protected by an armed working population? Or would they sabotage the economy?

The answer came only eight months after the Day of Joy. Ortega, as new Junta coordinator, almost immediately faced a political counterrevolution led

A Nicaraguan farmer is prepared for anything even as he works in his fields. During the 1980s, when U.S. president Ronald Reagan began funding the contras — an armed rebel movement that aimed to undermine the Sandinistas — some 100,000 Nicaraguans joined community militias for their own defense.

by a few of his supposed teammates. In early 1980, Edén Pastora, "Comandante Cero" of the National Palace raid, went to Costa Rica to take up arms against the Sandinistas. A month later, Junta members Violeta Chamorro and business mogul Robelo resigned, Chamorro citing health reasons and Robelo joining Pastora in Costa Rica. In November, the conservative elites' powerful COSEP (Superior Council of Private Enterprise) withdrew its six representatives from the Council of State, which ironically had been inaugurated in May to guarantee the revolution's broad alliance.

In 1981, the world press published a letter signed by four leading COSEP members in which they accused the government of creeping toward communism. They called for external intervention to prevent this. The four men were arrested for encouraging an invasion of their homeland.

By that time, U.S. president Reagan had started moving the contra invasion into high gear. Shuddering every time an airplane flew overhead, Nicaraguans were building air-raid shelters. More than 100,000 people joined community and workplace militias to safeguard their revolution. But the popular will meant nothing to the elites: They stepped up their political offensive, marching to the drumbeat of the escalating contra war.

As more foreign loans arrived, Ortega turned to the herculean task of jump-starting the economy in the midst of war. In the early 1980s, Nicaragua managed an astounding six percent annual growth rate, while its Latin American neighbors experienced negative economic growth. The Sandinista leaders' dialogue with workers and peasants gave citizens a feeling that they had a say in determining their own lives. Volunteer labor became common. Workers labored overtime to increase production. The government built 28,000 new homes for poor people. Agrarian reform distributed more than 6 million acres to 120,000 rural families and brought them electricity and drinking water. Under the guidance of Ortega's partner, Rosario Murillo, a cultural program brought movies, poetry, theatre, and art to people everywhere.

Reforms in health care were so dramatic that the World Health Organization declared Nicaragua a model for primary health care. Infant mortality decreased significantly as immunization programs wiped out measles and polio. By 1985, most Nicaraguans had access to medical care — many for the first time.

Labor union membership increased 10-fold, and social security was extended to cover twice as many workers as before. New laws gave women equal rights, and day-care centers became common. By 1985, women occupied 37 percent of FSLN leadership positions.

A pet project of both Ortega and his wife was the elimination of illiteracy among the poor. In 1980–81, more than 100,000 high school students and their teachers packed their knapsacks and hiked to the countryside to teach basic language and mathematics skills to old and young peasants by the light of kerosene lanterns. Half a million peasants became literate.

People from all over the world rushed to lend a hand. These internationalists included doctors, nurses, teachers, engineers, chemists, agronomists, musicians, farmers, students, and workers. More than 100,000 came from the United States.

Even floods in 1982 and a decision by cotton landowners to reduce production could not stop progress. But the contras could. As the Sandinista programs bore fruit, contra sabotage forced the government to shift its spending to military defense. A scandalous CIA manual for the contras was uncovered. It instructed Reagan's "freedom fighters" on techniques of sabotage and assassination.

> *The common people here were treated like dust before, deprived of all human rights, trampled by the aristocrats. Everything was for the benefit of a small upper class. This regime works the opposite way, gears itself to the rights and needs of the vast majority. Without a doubt this revolution incorporates the values of the gospel, Christian values.*
> —REV. JIM GOFF
> coordinator for the Committee
> of U.S. Citizens in Nicaragua

In the first half of the 1980s, the United States built several permanent military bases and stationed thousands of troops in Honduras. U.S. officials acknowledged that frequent military exercises and mock invasions near Nicaragua's borders were meant to harass the Sandinistas and prepare for a possible U.S. invasion. U.S. military strategists coined the term "low intensity conflict" to describe their operations, but the intensity was high for Nicaraguans. Former CIA director Stansfield Turner called U.S. policy "state-sponsored terrorism."

On March 25, 1982, Ortega appeared before the UN Security Council to urge an end to U.S. sponsorship of the contra war. While in New York, he received reports on the American people's anti-intervention movement.

Public opinion polls showed Americans opposing the war by a two-to-one margin. Mass protest demonstrations were occurring in several cities, as hundreds of thousands chanted "Hands off Nicaragua!" More than 1,000 American solidarity organizations had blossomed to defend human rights not only in Nicaragua but also in El Salvador, Guatemala, and Honduras. Some American towns had proclaimed themselves "sister cities" with Nicaraguan towns, collecting hundreds of thousands of dollars in material aid.

Ortega returned home filled with hope that the Americans' anti-intervention movement would grow as it had during the Vietnam War years. He remembered his father's story of the anti-imperialist movement in the United States that eventually helped Sandino terminate intervention in the 1920s and 1930s.

Congress responded to the pressure of public opinion in late 1982 by passing the Boland Amendment, barring the use of funds to overthrow the Nicaraguan government. That gave Ortega hope, although contra activities did not slow down. On the contrary, they sped up. Later, Ortega — and the entire world — would discover why the cutoff of funds to the contras had so little effect.

Seeking support for his unpopular policy, Reagan appointed a bipartisan commission to look into Central America. It was headed by former president

We have not come here to level accusations but to demand an end, once and for all, to the policy of aggression, threats, interventions, covert operations and invasions of our homeland and the region and to make it clear that the unfairly distributed resources of humanity on this planet do not give the right to act against weak and small peoples.

—DANIEL ORTEGA
speech to UN Security
Council, March 1982

Nixon's national security adviser Henry Kissinger.

Kissinger and his commission arrived in Managua in October 1983, five days after CIA operatives from offshore U.S. naval ships blew up oil storage tanks in the Nicaraguan harbor of Corinto. Ortega read a statement before the commission reviewing past and present U.S. crimes against Nicaragua. As usual, he refused to soften his words or be tactful. If Kissinger expected fawning humbleness, he did not receive it from Ortega.

Later, many in diplomatic circles claimed that Ortega had lost the possibility of winning over the Kissinger Commission with his "tactlessness." But others cited what happened to the U.S. ambassador Tony Quainton. CBS journalist and producer Peter Davis recounted the story. "Quainton advised the commission that the Nicaraguan government was not a dogmatic Soviet puppet . . . and [that] we should take their olive branches seriously. . . . Kissinger had disliked Ortega personally and was in no mood for this kind of conciliatory talk from Quainton. He told Reagan . . . to get rid of Tony." Not long afterwards, Quainton was removed from his post.

In October 1983, the United States invaded the Caribbean island of Grenada (population 100,000), ending Grenada's already faltering revolution of 1979. As Ambassador Quainton later told reporters, the Grenada invasion sent a clear message to the Nicaraguan government: "You could be next!"

Besides the American people's anti-intervention movement, Ortega had another hope for stopping U.S. aggression: the World Court. Nicaragua filed charges at the court after the CIA's 1983 mining of the harbors. Edgar Chamorro, a former contra public relations director and a distant cousin of the martyred editor of *La Prensa*, told the court that "hundreds of civilian murders, mutilations, tortures, and rapes" by the contras were committed "at the instigation of CIA-training officers." The United States had long championed the World Court as the backbone of international law. Now, realizing its case was weak, it withdrew its membership.

It was a deceptively deadly sparring match between a 1980s David and Goliath — a young Ortega and an aging Reagan. The American president

U.S. troops round up alleged members of the People's Revolutionary Army in Grenada. On October 25, 1983, Reagan ordered the invasion of the tiny Caribbean island, whose political instability he considered a threat to U.S. security. At least one journalist speculated that the invasion was to some extent intended as a warning to Nicaragua.

Ortega addresses the UN General Assembly in New York in September 1983. In his speech, he announced that his government had learned from reliable sources that the United States was planning an invasion of Nicaragua intended to interfere with scheduled free elections there.

sought to score a knockout by reshaping public opinion. He ordered military intelligence officers to carry out a covert propaganda operation to sell his policy to the American public. The much-publicized 1984 Kissinger Commission Report further helped soften opposition by recommending continued U.S. military aid to the contras.

Ortega sought to put an end to the sparring by endorsing a peace proposal that the Kissinger Commission Report had encouraged. On September 21, 1984, he offered to sign the so-called Contadora Peace Plan as put forward by Colombia, Mexico, Panama, and Venezuela and modified by the United States. Contadora called for demilitarization, pluralism, and democratic elections in every Central American country.

Reagan rejected Ortega's offer. In the *New York Times* of September 24, 1984, correspondent Philip Taubman quoted a State Department official as saying, "The whole point was to get the Nicaraguans to accept the Contadora proposals. Now they have, but we say we aren't satisfied. I'm not sure I would blame the Nicaraguans if they were confused."

Ortega was not confused. He knew full well that the Reagan administration did not want the Sandinista government legitimized by free elections. A U.S. National Security Council (NSC) document, later leaked to the *Washington Post*, boasted "We have effectively blocked Contadora Group efforts."

On October 2, 1984, Ortega addressed the UN General Assembly. He informed the world that intelligence information had revealed a U.S. plan for a two-front invasion to force the Nicaraguan government to cancel its November 4 elections. Ortega believed the invasion plan was later scrapped because of his exposure and the outraged response of many Americans.

While in New York, Ortega accepted a pair of eyeglasses as a gift from wealthy American friends. New York's newspapers ran stories that the president of poverty-stricken Nicaragua had spent more than $3,000 on eyeglasses for himself and his family. Whether the glasses actually cost that much was never verified, but Ortega definitely had not known the monetary value of the gift. Shocked by the headlines, Rosario Murillo exclaimed, "I never dreamed glasses would cost so much . . . and we hadn't paid a cent."

On November 4, 1984, Nicaragua successfully carried out its first democratic elections in history. An election observation team sent by the Latin American Studies Association (LASA), the largest organization of experts on Latin America in the United States, declared them "a model of probity and fairness."

During the campaign, Ortega seemed incapable of the usual behavior of politicians. People called him Daniel, and children reached out to touch him. He smiled only when he meant it, and he neither kissed babies nor hugged young women. He spoke honestly and made no false promises. One unsympathetic author commented caustically, "Ortega at 22 on his way to prison was what he remained at 38 . . . a man obsessed with his nation."

Most Nicaraguans were not displeased by Ortega's so-called obsession. The president of the most powerful nation in the world had called their homeland a "Marxist dungeon." Nicaragua was in a highly dangerous and vulnerable situation, and it fell to Ortega to navigate his country through shark-filled waters.

Seven political parties ran candidates in the elections, and Ortega won the presidency with two-thirds of the vote. He took the oath of office on January 10, 1985.

Ortega is greeted by children during the 1984 campaign for the presidency. By all accounts, Ortega ran an honest, positive campaign, making no empty promises.

In November 1984, Ortega became president of Nicaragua in the country's first free election. He took the oath of office on January 10, 1985. A governing body, the National Assembly, was also elected, and a new constitution was drafted. Democracy seemed to be taking root in Nicaragua.

Nicaragua's newly elected parliament, the National Assembly, began debating the nation's future. More than a third of its members were opponents of the Sandinistas, including some outspoken contra supporters. The Assembly drafted a new constitution, promulgated on January 9, 1987. Of the Assembly's 22-member Constitutional Commission, 8 were FSLN members.

As approved, the constitution guaranteed "political pluralism, the mixed economy, and nonalignment." It also protected the revolution's gains: agrarian reform; nationalization of banks and foreign trade; rights of labor, women, and ethnic minorities; freedom of speech and assembly; regular free elections; and the Sandinista People's Army. Private religious education was allowed, but church and state were kept separate.

Ortega could rightfully feel proud of the revolution's many accomplishments enshrined in the 1987 constitution. But he was not a boastful man. In fact, he readily acknowledged that the revolution had more than once stumbled badly. As he told CBS news writer Peter Davis, "We've made our errors, mistakes on the Atlantic Coast . . . censorship . . . the relationship with the church."

The mistake on the Atlantic Coast was the government's forcible removal of Miskito Indians from the war zone along the Honduran border. The world-renowned human rights organization Amnesty International concluded, however, that Sandinista violations of Miskito rights were nothing compared to those committed by the contras. Nicaragua's 1987 constitution set a Latin American "first" by granting local autonomy to all Indian groups.

Ortega's reference to censorship involved *La Prensa*, whose editors publicly acknowledged they received a CIA subsidy. Because the CIA was waging a war against Nicaragua and *La Prensa* frequently published seditious material, the government periodically censored it.

Mistakes concerning the church were less serious in Ortega's eyes. A few priests were deported because of their counterrevolutionary activities. Three priests, advocates of liberation theology, served as top officials in Ortega's administration. In 1985, the pope ordered them to resign, saying that religion must not be political. They refused, asking the pope why he had said nothing about Archbishop Obando y Bravo's political activities. Obando y Bravo told U.S. businesspeople right before the 1984 elections that he and his diocese were actively involved in efforts to topple the government. Later, a captured video showed one of the archbishop's priests cursing the Sandinista leaders as he shared drinks with CIA agents.

Time after time, Ortega explained to visiting Americans the differences between the Sandinista view of democratic freedoms and the U.S. view. Ortega emphasized freedom for the individual but not if it meant freedom to exploit others. "Your freedom, sir, is a monster," he told Davis. "The result of the kind of economic freedom that existed under Somoza was [that] it satisfied a few individuals at the expense of all other individuals. We don't want the democracy of oppression and the freedom of exploitation that Washington wants to impose on us. *Nunca. Nunca.* Never."

Ortega's anger was understandable. Despite free elections and compromises with Nicaragua's businesspeople, the contra war did not abate. For Ortega and the vast majority of Nicaraguans, the American concept of freedom was contradicted by the terrorism of the U.S.-commanded contras, whose attacks became even more widespread after Nicaraguans exercised their hard-won right to vote in 1984.

Many Nicaraguans, including Ortega, remembered a poem called "To Roosevelt," written by Nicaraguan poet Rubén Darío, who disliked the U.S. penchant for bullying its neighbors. Darío died in 1916, but his words are still timely:

> You are the United States,
> future invader of our naive America.
> Roosevelt, you must become, by God's will,
> the deadly Rifleman and the dreadful Hunter
> before you can clutch us in your iron claws.

Nicaraguans needed only to substitute the name *Reagan* for *Roosevelt* to fit Darío's poem to the 1980s.

Respect for the sovereignty of our countries has never been obtained from the United States. The expansionist thinking of the last century, the gunboat treaties, the big-stick policy, have emerged again. . . . Let the forces of reason and love, the forces of peace, triumph once again over the irrational forces.
—DANIEL ORTEGA
speech to UN General
Assembly, October 1981

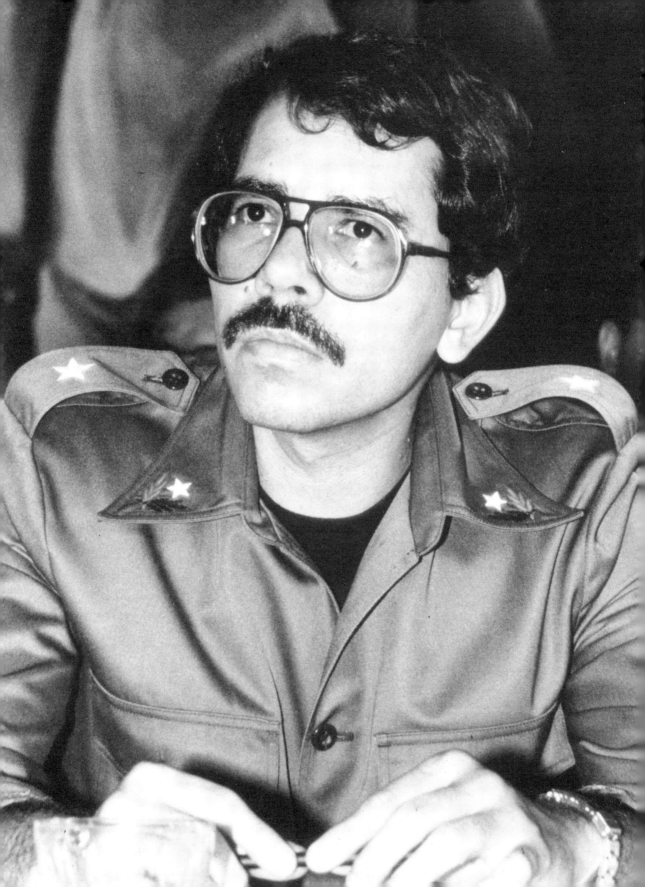

7

Long Arm of the Yankees

On May 1, 1985, President Ortega faced a new act of U.S. aggression — an economic embargo declared by President Reagan. It violated international law and cut Nicaragua off from obtaining foods and other basic goods from its largest supplier, the United States. In 1986 the U.S. Congress narrowly approved a contra-aid package of $100 million. By May 1987, annual U.S. troop "exercises" in Honduras and off Nicaragua's coasts involved more than 50,000 U.S. military personnel.

Ortega was well aware that the U.S. war was a secret "dirty war" involving thousands of U.S. combatants — some of them died inside Nicaraguan territory. From 1981 to 1989, a U.S. "secret army" of the SOD (Special Operations Division of the U.S. Army) carried out several military actions in Nicaragua. In 1983, the Associated Press wire service reported 17 fatalities suffered in Nicaragua by the 160th Task Force of the 101st Airborne Division, a U.S. Army helicopter unit.

Communism was not your enemy. Our independence was your enemy.
—DANIEL ORTEGA
on U.S. involvement in
Central America

When Ortega took office, U.S. aggression toward the Sandinistas intensified. The Reagan administration and the U.S. Congress approved a $100-million contra aid package, and some 50,000 U.S. military personnel engaged in exercises off the Nicaraguan coast.

Maurice Ortega and his father relax with the newspaper at home in 1987. The Ortegas have nine children.

Throughout these terrible times, Ortega lived with his family in a simple rambling bungalow in a residential section of Managua. The house was hidden behind high cement walls, with armed guards stationed every few feet. Inside the compound, flowers, trees, and sidewalks provided a pleasant environment where the children could play. By 1987, 9 Ortega children lived there, ranging in age from infancy to 22 (the older ones from Rosario Murillo's earlier marriage). Two "nannies" and housekeepers helped care for the house and children while Murillo worked full-time. Inside the house, American rock music poured from the children's bedrooms. Paintings by Murillo's artist friends adorned the walls, as well as family photographs — including one of Ortega and Fidel Castro with baseballs and bats. A family dog raced through piles of scattered toys. Children in pajamas and T-shirts were everywhere, giggling and chattering.

It was a valiant effort at normalcy, but the whole household lived in fear. Sandinista bodyguards were always present. The reason was that in 1986 the U.S. government had declared Libyan President Muammar El-Qaddafi a "terrorist" and had sent planes to bomb his home, killing Qaddafi's infant daughter. Ortega had met Qaddafi during one of his many trips requesting loans for Nicaragua and had obtained $100 million. He felt that might be the real reason for the raid on Libya, and he worried that his own home might be the next target.

The Ortegas were particularly concerned about their son Carlos Enrique, called "Tino" by his family, who was about 10 at the time of the raid on Libya. "Every time we went out," Rosario Murillo told a reporter, "he would be calling us every five minutes asking, 'What time will you be coming back. I'm scared that you'll get killed. I'm scared that my father will get killed.' " He told his mother, "I know I'm going to die very young." Murillo comforted him as best she could and told interviewers, "We smile here. You can't just feel like the world is on top of you. . . . Daniel is a person who always has the ability to find a way out, to find the good side, to make things better."

Things did look a little better in 1986 when the World Court censured the United States as a criminal aggressor on 15 counts of international law. The court called for an immediate end of U.S. aid to the contras and their "acts contrary to general principles of humanitarian law"; damage payments to Nicaragua; and lifting of the trade embargo. The United States refused to recognize the decision, and the war continued unabated.

In October 1986, Nicaraguan teenagers aimed their shoulder-braced rocket launchers at a low-flying U.S. cargo plane carrying arms for a drop to some contras. The plane crashed in the jungle, killing all of its American crew members except one. The next day, newspapers all over the world showed a handcuffed U.S. cargo handler, Eugene Hasenfus, being taken prisoner. Ortega, in one of his typical conciliatory gestures, had Hasenfus released.

But now the "secret war" was public. During the next four years, one of the biggest scandals in U.S. political history unfolded — "Iran-contragate." It turned out that, in order to circumvent the 1982 Boland Amendment, the Reagan administration had sold weapons to the Iranian government of Ayatollah Khomeini (whom it accused of being a "terrorist") and then used the profits to arm, feed, and clothe the contras. In directing the operation from the White House basement, NSC staff member Lieutenant Colonel Oliver North oversaw a wide network of arms dealers and secret bank accounts. From North, the chain of command looped through the CIA, the NSC (where Vice-president George Bush sat), and on up to President Reagan, who in 1990 said the operation had been undertaken "at my behest."

Ortega realized, of course, that the shooting down of Hasenfus's plane set the stage for the U.S. Congress to hold hearings and collect volumes of testimony and depositions on Iran-contragate. He hoped its hearings would shock the American public into insisting on an end to the war.

The hearings revealed that the Reagan-Bush administration had contingency plans to suspend the U.S. Constitution and to use already con-

Eugene Hasenfus, a Wisconsin man who was caught running guns to the contras when his C-123 transport plane crashed 25 miles north of the Costa Rica border, is held prisoner by a Sandinista soldier on October 7, 1986.

U.S. president Ronald Reagan meets with contra representatives (from left) Arturo Cruz, Adolfo Calero, and Alfonso Robelo at the White House in March 1986. When Congress cut off funds to the contras, the Reagan administration devised a plan to do it illegally. The result: The Iran-contra scandal.

structed "detention centers" as holding pens for up to 400,000 protesters in the event of a U.S. invasion of Nicaragua — the invasion Ortega had long warned against. Iran-contragate implicated the U.S. executive branch of government in a long list of criminal activities, including obstruction of justice, violations of the arms export and neutrality acts, planning assassinations of foreign leaders, and the overriding of Congress's right to declare war.

Ironically, only months before the scandal broke, President Reagan went on national television with photographs ostensibly showing members of Ortega's administration loading narcotics onto airplanes at Managua's airport for transport to the United States. An embarrassed Drug Enforcement Administration (DEA) had to announce the next day that the president's charge was false. In fact, Iran-contragate revelations showed that the North-contra operation was bringing back cocaine and marijuana in the planes that dropped arms to the contras, using drug profits to help fund the war. The two key airfields used were Florida's Homestead Air Force Base and the 1,750-acre Costa Rican ranch of CIA agent John Hull (who sometimes conferred with future Vice-president Dan Quayle). Even worse, evidence showed that North, the FBI, the Department of Justice, and the DEA blocked further investigation into the drug running. Vice-president Bush, heading up the "war on drugs" at the time, looked the other way. President Reagan ordered executive agencies not to deliver documents to a Senate committee investigating the impact of narcotics trafficking on U.S. policy.

To Ortega's pleasant surprise, Vietnam War veterans instantly responded to Iran-contragate, comparing the barbaric acts of the U.S. military and contras in Nicaragua to what they had been ordered to do in Vietnam. They pointed out that Oliver North had gone on television during the Vietnam War to defend the massacres of entire village populations like the highly publicized one at My Lai. In 1988, a "Vietnam Veterans' Convoy" of 37 trucks reached the Nicaraguan border and delivered food, medicine, and clothing. The veterans, along with many other Americans, agreed with President Kennedy's former national security adviser McGeorge Bundy that it was "genuinely zany" to think that tiny Nicaragua could threaten national security, as Reagan claimed. Even more important was the question of whether the United States had the right to interfere in the revolutions of small nations in order to protect the profits of U.S. corporations.

Ortega was grateful to the veterans. He never made the mistake of equating the U.S. government with the American people. He often spoke of his friendship for Americans, especially the internationalists. One of them, engineer Ben Linder, was gunned down in 1987 by a contra raid on a cooperative farm where he had been helping to build a hydroelectric project. His brother went on American television to state that Ben had been killed by the U.S. government, citing President Reagan's 1985 boast "I am a contra."

But Ortega did not get everything he hoped for from the congressional hearings. Oliver North became a TV celebrity, known affectionately as Ollie. Had not Ortega's father once told him how an earlier Yanquis mercenary, William Walker, had won popularity in America? Moreover, as several senators and representatives later acknowledged, Congress "covered up" much of the sordid story of Iran-contragate, fearing it would weaken the presidency too much.

> *If the United States had worried once, only one time, about democracy during all its invasions of Central America and of Nicaragua in particular, if the United States had used the postulates of Jefferson on democracy and applied them here, there would never have been the need for violent revolution in Nicaragua, nor in El Salvador, nor Guatemala nor anywhere else.*
> —DANIEL ORTEGA

Ortega accompanies the family of 27-year-old engineer Benjamin Linder, a U.S. citizen living in Nicaragua, who was killed by contras on April 28, 1987. Linder's murder contributed to Congress's decision to cut off aid to the rebel forces.

More shocking revelations came out in 1990 when a jury acquitted former CIA arms contract agent Richard Brenneke of the charge that he had lied about his detailed knowledge of a 1980 Reagan-Bush campaign arrangement with Iran to postpone release of American hostages until after President Carter lost the election. In other words, had the hostages been released earlier Carter might have won the 1980 elections and spared Nicaragua a decade of war and destruction — something Ortega had initially expected from a Carter presidency.

As Ortega sadly knew, the victims of Reagan's election and Iran-contragate were the Nicaraguan people. By 1990, he said, the contra war had claimed 60,000 lives. U.S. sources put the toll at 30,000. There was hardly a Nicaraguan who did not have at least one dead or wounded relative.

To make matters worse, Nicaragua's economy ground to a halt. To fund the war, President Ortega had to cut back social programs. Between 1986 and 1987, he announced an end to all housing construction and wage hikes and implemented an economic austerity plan favoring private investors. To survive, Nicaraguans began taking extra jobs and turning to the black market for scarce goods. The government had to borrow more money, and the foreign debt ballooned to four times what the economy could produce in a single year. In 1988, citizens cut their consumption of milk by half, and the number of infants dying from diarrhea doubled. Rising prices pushed the inflation rate to a peak of 30,000 percent. Nicaraguans were going hungry. The situation was becoming desperate.

To end the U.S. war and economic embargo that was destroying his homeland, Ortega undertook a triple offensive: military counterattack, support for a new peace plan, and the holding of Nicaragua's second democratic national elections, in 1990. In 1984, he announced a military draft of all males ages 18 to 25 to serve 2 years' active duty. Nicaraguans had never known a draft, and some resented it.

Starting in late 1985, the draftees' BLIs (Irregular Fight Batallions of 1,000 men) began establishing military superiority over the contras. Aided by Soviet-built MI-24 and MI-8 helicopters, they were able to make entire zones "contra-free." In Costa Rica,

A Nicaraguan family, rendered homeless by the civil war between the Sandinista government and the U.S.-backed contra rebels, awaits a fate unknown at a relocation camp in a remote village some 150 miles southeast of Managua.

Edén Pastora stopped fighting after the CIA broke with him because of his refusal to unite with known torturers who led the main contra army based in Honduras.

By 1987, Ortega felt he had the contras on the run. They had not won an inch of Nicaraguan territory and had lost more than 12,000 men in battle. Ortega spoke of a "strategic defeat of the contras." Contra leaders admitted they could not win.

On August 7, 1987, Ortega and the other four Central American presidents signed in Guatemala the Arias Peace Plan, which earned Costa Rican president Oscar Arias Sánchez the Nobel Peace Prize. Picking up from where the stalled Contadora process had left off, the Arias Peace Plan called for cease-fires, peace negotiations, amnesties for armed opposition groups and political prisoners, political pluralism, democratic elections, and a cutoff in outside aid to rebels, especially aid to the contras. Ortega declared a cease-fire in April 1988 and gave amnesty to returning contras.

Nearly a million Nicaraguans rallied on July 19, 1989, to celebrate the revolution's 10th anniversary. The next month, Ortega persuaded the other Central American presidents in Tela, Honduras, to sign the Tela Accords. These called for the complete disbanding of the contras by December 5. At home, Ortega continued promoting a conciliatory policy for business owners, now calling it *concertación*, or coming together.

In October 1989, at the first hemispheric summit meeting of presidents in 22 years, held in San José, Costa Rica, President Ortega and President Bush presented contrasting images to the world's press. Ortega maintained his dignity. But Bush repeatedly lost control, calling Ortega "this little man" and confusing him with Panama's General Manuel Noriega. Bush reportedly called Ortega "an unwanted animal at a garden party."

The December 5 deadline for contra demobilization passed with little letup in contra military attacks. One of them killed an American nun in January 1990. A couple of months before Nicaragua's 1990 election, the United States launched an-

Ortega holds on his shoulder Miss 10th Anniversary, 10-year-old Yahira Magaly Gonzalez, at the celebration of the 10th anniversary of the Sandinista revolution. The girl was born in 1979, the year the Somoza regime was toppled.

other full-scale invasion of Panama. The sneak attack at midnight took hundreds, perhaps thousands of Panamanian lives and led to the capture of Noriega, who had stopped cooperating with U.S. military operations against Nicaragua a few years earlier. Accorded official "prisoner of war" status, Noriega was incarcerated in Florida to await U.S. trial on drug-dealing charges. Meanwhile, President Bush increased his pressure on Ortega to release remaining political prisoners before the 1990 elections.

Ortega again responded with a conciliatory gesture, even though the contras had not stuck by their promise to disband. In January 1990, he released all but a few of Nicaragua's remaining 1,306 political prisoners. Most of the freed men were contras, and a few were former members of the National Guard. Ortega remained stone faced when it was announced that among those released were the assassins of his brother Camilo and of FSLN founder Carlos Fonseca.

U.S. soldiers and heavy artillery cut an imposing figure on the landscape of Panama during the U.S. invasion of that country in December 1989. The invasion culminated in the capture of former CIA informant General Manuel Noriega.

8

To the Mountains Again?

Daniel Ortega began his 1990 reelection campaign filled with optimism. The contra war was winding down, and thousands of peasant contras had accepted his amnesty to return to their families. Public opinion polls had him comfortably leading his opponent, the candidate of the revived 14-party National Opposition Union (UNO), Violeta Chamorro, the gray-haired widow of the popular martyred journalist.

Ortega had arranged for scrupulously fair elections. This was confirmed by 2,000 official foreign observers, including 3 teams he personally had invited from the OAS, the United Nations, and the Carter Center (of former president Carter). Using the slogan "Everything's going to be better," Ortega expected that a second Sandinista election victory — with respected international observers on hand — would finally force the U.S. government to end its war.

> On February 25, the Sandinistas and all Nicaraguan people offered a great lesson in democracy. We Sandinistas are proud to be the basis, the foundation, the main pillar of democracy in Nicaragua, because democracy in Nicaragua cannot be understood without "Sandinismo" nor "Sandinismo" without democracy.
>
> —DANIEL ORTEGA
> after the defeat of the Sandinistas by the National Opposition party in the 1990 elections

Ortega, with his son Camilo, campaigns for reelection in 1990. Having spent his entire adult life in the service of his country, Ortega — student activist, guerrilla fighter, head of the revolutionary junta, and the first legitimate president of Nicaragua — was favored to defeat his opponent in the election, Violeta Chamorro.

Nicaraguan election officials discuss the balloting process with former U.S. attorney general Elliot Richardson. Richardson was among some 2,000 foreigners who were invited to observe the February 1990 presidential election in Nicaragua.

But many Nicaraguan voters wondered if Bush would accept an Ortega victory. Had not Reagan refused to recognize Ortega's 1984 election? Indeed, having so readily taken over Panama, would not Bush be more likely to deny an Ortega win and escalate his military pressures? As if to drive the point home, the contras grew more bold in their actions during the election campaign, killing 200 people, most of them civilians.

Some Nicaraguans said that spending scarce resources on elections in an effort to turn back U.S. criticisms was a waste of time. No matter what the Sandinistas did, they would be called "Marxist-Leninists" by Bush. Better to be hung by a wolf than a lamb, said these critics. They charged that Ortega's gentle handling of big business interests had made it easier for the elite to destabilize the economy. In their view, Ortega should have announced that new elections could not be held until the contras were demobilized, the trade embargo lifted, war reparations paid, and Nicaragua's economy given a chance to recover. Other critics asserted that the only way for Nicaragua to be independent from "the long arm of the Yankees" was to give workers and peasants more control and to push for a socialist Nicaragua and a unified socialist Central America.

Ortega's supporters responded that his more moderate approach had helped win European support. Holding elections, they said, helped the FSLN to raise the consciousness of the masses who were being swamped with church and "proimperialist" propaganda. They told their revolutionary brethren that people were not yet ready for socialism, which had to be created in stages.

Like Ortega, UNO candidate Chamorro campaigned for peace. She openly welcomed the support of President Bush, leaving the impression that if the war was U.S.-caused, then obviously a friend of the American president could end it more quickly than his known enemy.

Throngs of townspeople wearing pro-FSLN T-shirts and caps accompany Ortega as he campaigns astride a white horse in the village of Dario, Nicaragua, in January 1990. Around his neck, the candidate wears the traditional red-and-black scarf of the Sandinistas.

The National Opposition Union (UNO) candidate Violeta Chamorro, confined to a wheelchair because of a kneecap fracture, campaigns vigorously nonetheless. Implicitly referring to the candidate's martyred husband, one UNO official said of her, "She is a symbol . . . not of the past, or the present, or even the future. She is a symbol of what might have been."

Chamorro's campaign was well funded. Besides contributions from the big capitalists and the contras' war chest, she drew on $9.1 million voted by the U.S. Congress to "assist Nicaragua in its elections." This was in addition to the $3.5 million sent in 1989 and almost $5 million spent by the CIA for the opposition parties. U.S. support for Chamorro's UNO thus ran as high as $10 per Nicaraguan voter, roughly 30 times what George Bush had spent per voter in his presidential campaign. The Latin American tradition of buying poor people's votes helped tilt the balance in Chamorro's favor.

Almost everyone agreed that Nicaraguans voted for the candidate they thought would best be able to end, in sociologist Carlos Vilas' words, "a decade of counterrevolutionary war that left thousands dead, wounded and crippled . . . and basic goods in desperately short supply."

At 11:30 P.M. on election day, Ortega invited the OAS, UN, and Carter observer teams to meet with him. They told the press the next day that a stunned Nicaraguan president had gracefully acknowledged his defeat. The Carter Center observer team started setting up meetings between representatives of Chamorro and Ortega to arrange for a peaceful transfer of power.

Most Nicaraguans did not know about the election results until the day after they voted, when they woke up to see their president on national television conceding defeat. Ortega had lost by 13 percentage points, and the Sandinistas had won in only two zones: the northern Estelí area and the South Atlantic region. But UNO did not have the two-thirds of the Assembly needed to amend the Constitution. Ortega promised to "respect and comply" with the election results and called for "the consolidation of democracy."

A Nicaraguan woman goes through an agonizing decision-making process at the ballot box while her baby is tended to by an election assistant. When the votes were tallied, Ortega was defeated.

The first day after the election was like a day of national mourning. There were no wild celebrations in the streets. It was as if Nicaraguans had voted for Chamorro only because they felt it was the best chance for getting the United States to end its embargo and war. That same day the Bush administration announced they would do exactly that. The American president said that "there is no reason at all for further military activity from any quarter." The man who a few months earlier had called Ortega "an animal" now commended him for his statesmanlike behavior.

That evening, Ortega visited Chamorro to discuss the transition. She reportedly greeted him with the words "My beautiful little father, come in because I love you," to which Ortega replied "You know that I respect you and love you and congratulate you on your triumph." They then hugged each other.

Next day, Chamorro gave her acceptance speech. Ruling out vengeance, she affirmed: "This election will produce no exiles, no political prisoners, no confiscations." She declared a general amnesty and called for the "rapid and immediate" demobilization of the contras.

Two days after the election, nearly 200,000 people overflowed Managua's Omar Torrijos and Non-Aligned plazas to cheer Ortega. Promising that the FSLN would be "a constructive but belligerent opposition force," Ortega vowed to defend the mixed economy and the right to strike — important gains made by the Sandinistas. He predicted that many people who voted out of desperation for UNO "will soon join us and vote for the Front from below. . . . We will continue governing from below." Then he added:"We were sure we were going to die in the struggle (against Somoza III). We never imagined we would make it to see the triumph. We were not born at the top, we were born at the bottom and we are used to fighting from below. . . . We are used to struggling in the face of our executioners and torturers. So now that people's power, revolutionary power exists in this country, we have much better conditions in the short term to return to governing from above."

I want to confirm that this election will produce no exiles, no political prisoners, no confiscations. There are no winners or losers.
—VIOLETA BARRIOS DE CHAMORRO
in her acceptance speech after the February 1990 elections

On April 25, 1990, Ortega passed the presidency to Chamorro at Managua's 28,000-seat baseball stadium. Wearing red-and-black scarves, Sandinistas filled the seats from behind third base to the left-field bleachers. On the right side behind the first base line sat Chamorro's supporters waving blue-and-white UNO flags.

Back in Washington, President Bush signed a formal determination that Nicaragua was no longer "a Marxist-Leninist country" and asked Congress to approve a $300 million aid package that included

In Managua, 2 days after the election, some 200,000 people came out to pay tribute to Daniel Ortega. Because he had led his country down the road to freedom and had given Nicaraguans hope for a brighter future, Ortega received a hero's farewell.

$47 million for the contras' resettlement. Congress voted for the aid and Bush signed it into law on May 26, 1990. Much of the money went to service Nicaragua's debt. About $128 million of it was earmarked for restoring "the productive capacity of the Nicaraguan economy." *La Prensa*, apparently still unable to publish without a CIA or other U.S. subsidy, received $125,000. Another $100,000 went to tiny CIA-linked trade unions.

In April, because contra leaders broke an agreement to disarm before Chamorro's inauguration, the Sandinistas' labor confederation launched a national strike. It ended only after the contras accepted a June 10 demobilization deadline under UN supervision.

Thus, as president, Chamorro came face to face with people's expectations for maintaining the revolution's gains. With one hand she sought to appease the Sandinistas by retaining Humberto Ortega as defense minister, who in turn agreed to a one-third cut in army personnel (from 60,000 to 40,000). With the other hand she began reversing Sandinista programs by creating a "super ministry" to start selling off state properties. Her government started returning or paying compensation for confiscated lands. It devalued the Nicaraguan basic unit of currency, the cordoba, by 300 percent in 10 days and allowed sharp price increases. Perhaps most controversial was President Chamorro's suspension of a civil service law that granted job protection to state workers. A week-long strike by thousands of civil service and public transport workers in mid-May 1990 won reinstatement of the law and the doubling of wages that in the future will be required to keep pace with inflation.

When rising prices again raced ahead of wages 6 weeks later, the Sandinistas declared a general strike that drew the support of many university and high school students and paralyzed the nation for 10 days. Government supporters shot at strikers, who put up street barricades; at least four people were killed. The army and police watched nervously. According to some members of the U.S. Congress, infantry troops at California's Fort Ord (who had

> *Forward, forward with our struggle, with our call to arms which is Sandino's cry: "Patria Libre o Morir!"*
>
> —DANIEL ORTEGA
> in the closing of his
> concession speech after the
> February 1990 elections

participated in the 1989 Panama invasion) were placed on a 15-minute alert to be rushed to Nicaragua.

In the midst of this precarious situation, Ortega and other Sandinistas patiently negotiated an agreement with the Chamorro administration. The government made major concessions. It granted wage increases and promised to establish a new national minimum wage, as well as to consult union representatives in designing its economic recovery program in industry and public transportation. It also agreed to stop returning confiscated lands. Here was a striking example of what Ortega meant by Sandinista "governing from below."

Meanwhile, as contra leaders continued sabotaging agreements to disarm, the Chamorro government — itself badly divided — made a new agreement with them. The agreement set up "development poles," or areas in southeastern Nicaragua where the contras could receive land, economic aid, and social services. A new police force to patrol the contra zones would include former contra commandos. Sandinista civilian militias stationed in the areas would have to disarm.

Ortega watched these developments with great concern. Would the armed contras in the new police force become "death squads"? Now that Honduras said it would host no more contras, would southeastern Nicaragua become the new launching pad for war?

Before Somoza had been driven from Nicaragua, Ortega had known only jails, safe houses, and the uncertain life of an underground guerrilla fighter seeking to fulfill Sandino's dream of "a free homeland or death." Now he confronted the future, still dreaming, still fighting, still alive.

Would new battles be necessary to free his homeland from "the long arm of the Yankees?" Would he, like the Nicaraguans of Sandino's time, again have to "go to the mountains"? Those who knew Ortega believed that was the *last* thing he wanted to do. But if it became necessary for the revolution, they said, you could count on one thing — Daniel Ortega would not hesitate to take up arms again.

A pensive Ortega watches as Violeta Chamorro is inaugurated president of Nicaragua. Whether the Chamorro administration will be successful and whether the world has seen the last of Daniel Ortega remains to be seen.

Further Reading

Bigelow, William, and Jeff Edmundson, eds. *Inside the Volcano: A Curriculum on Nicaragua.* Washington, DC: Network of Educators' Committees on Central America, 1990.

Cabestrero, Teofilo. *Ministers of God, Ministers of the People.* Maryknoll, NY: Orbis Books, 1983.

Cabezas, Omar. *Fire from the Mountain: The Making of a Sandinista.* New York: Crown, 1985.

Central Intelligence Agency. *The Freedom Fighter's Manual.* New York: Grove, 1985.

Chomsky, Noam. *Turning the Tide: U.S. Intervention in Central America and the Struggle for Peace.* Boston: South End Press, 1986.

Cockburn, Leslie. *Out of Control: The Story of the Reagan Administration's Secret War in Nicaragua, the Illegal Arms Pipeline, and the Contra Drug Connection.* Boston: Atlantic Monthly Press, 1987.

Cockcroft, James D. *Neighbors in Turmoil: Latin America.* New York: HarperCollins, 1989.

Davis, Peter. *Where Is Nicaragua?* New York: Simon & Schuster, 1987.

Gilbert, Dennis. *Sandinistas.* New York: Blackwell, 1988.

Gutman, Roy. *Banana Diplomacy: The Making of American Policy in Nicaragua 1981–1987.* New York: Simon & Schuster, 1987.

Heyck, Denis Lynn Daly. *Life Stories of the Nicaraguan Revolution.* New York: Routledge, Chapman & Hall, 1990.

Meiselas, Susan. *Nicaragua in Photographs.* New York: Pantheon, 1981.

Nolan, David. *The Ideology of the Sandinistas and the Nicaraguan Revolution.* Coral Gables, FL: Institute of Interamerican Studies, 1984.

Ruchwager, Gary. *People in Power: Forging a Grassroots Democracy in Nicaragua.* South Hadley, MA: Bergin & Garvey, 1987.

Ruis. *Nicaragua for Beginners.* New York: Writers & Readers, 1984.

Rushdie, Salman. *The Jaguar Smile: A Nicaraguan Journey.* New York: Viking, 1987.

Sklar, Holly. *Washington's War on Nicaragua.* Boston: South End Press, 1988.

Somoza, Anastasio. *Nicaragua Betrayed.* Boston: Western Islands Publishing, 1980.

White, Steven. *Culture and Politics in Nicaragua: Testimonies of Poets and Writers.* New York: Lumen Books, 1986.

Chronology

Nov. 11, 1945	Born Daniel Jose Ortega Saavedra in La Libertad, Chontales, Nicaragua
1960	Joins Nicaraguan Patriotic Youth; arrested for political activity
1963	Leaves law school to join FSLN and becomes leader of anti-Somoza group
1967	Imprisoned after bank robbery; convicted and sentenced to eight years in jail
1967–74	Coordinates prisoner education and nationwide prisoner defense campaigns while incarcerated
Dec. 1974	Christmas raid in Managua; Ortega freed and flown to Cuba
1974–76	Member of National Directorate FSLN; with brother Humberto Ortega forms Tercerista Tendency
Jan. 10, 1978	Pedro Joaquín Chamorro assassinated; anti-Somoza protests intensify
1979	Ortega named coordinator of Junta of National Reconstruction; Day of Joy (July 19): Sandinistas march into Managua two days after Somoza flees
1980	Violeta Chamorro and Alfonso Robelo resign from Junta; first attacks by U.S.-backed anti-Sandinista forces (the contras)
1981	Ronald Reagan inaugurated U.S. president; U.S. Congress approves $19 million in aid for the contras
1983	House votes to end aid to the contras
1984	CIA involved in the mining of Nicaraguan harbors; Ortega elected president of Nicaragua
1986	Eugene Hasenfus captured when U.S.-manned cargo plane is shot down, implicating CIA in contra-supply operations; U.S. attorney general Edwin Meese admits profits from the sale of arms to Iran were diverted to the Nicaraguan contras
1988	Ortega declares cease-fire in contra war
1989	Five Central American presidents call for the demobilization of the contras
1990	Ortega defeated in presidential election by opposition coalition leader Violeta Chamorro; Sandinistas win week-long strike against Chamorro government's antilabor acts; Congress approves $300 million aid package for Nicaragua; Ortega helps negotiate an agreement with Chamorro government that ends return of confiscated lands and gives labor a bigger voice in the country's future

Index

James D. Cockcroft is a visiting professor at the State University of New York at Albany. A three-time Fulbright scholar, he is a consulting editor for the Chelsea House series HISPANICS OF ACHIEVEMENT and has written numerous books and articles on Latin American history and politics, including *Neighbors in Turmoil: Latin America.*

Arthur M. Schlesinger, jr., taught history at Harvard for many years and is currently Albert Schweitzer Professor of the Humanities at City University of New York. He is the author of numerous highly praised works in American history and has twice been awarded the Pulitzer Prize. He served in the White House as special assistant to Presidents Kennedy and Johnson.

PICTURE CREDITS

AP/Wide World Photos: pp. 29, 36, 39, 41, 45, 53, 58, 66, 69, 72, 86; Borrell/Sipa Press: pp. 12, 74; Alain Dejean/Sygma: p. 73; Bill Gentile/Sipa Press: pp. 98, 101; Diego Goldberg/Sygma: p. 2; Instituto de Historia de Nicaragua: pp. 35, 40, 47, 50, 61, 68, 71; Courtesy of the Jimmy Carter Library: p. 77; Library of Congress: pp. 24, 32; Susan Meiselas/Magnum: pp. 14, 16, 90, 103, 107; Chris Poveda/Sipa Press: pp. 80, 88; Reuters/Bettmann Archive: pp. 94, 95, 96, 97, 102, 105; Ivo Saglietti/Sipa Press: p. 85; Chris Simon-pietri/Sygma: p. 62; Trippett/Sipa Press: p. 92; UN photo 157237: p. 100; UN photo 162086/Yukata Nagata: p. 84; UPI/Bettmann Archive: pp. 17, 21, 33, 34, 38, 43, 44, 56, 57, 60, 70, 76, 78, 83, 91